Lean Government

By Ade Asefeso MCIPS MBA

Copyright 2014 by Ade Asefeso MCIPS MBA
All rights reserved.

First Edition

ISBN-13: 978-1503380240

ISBN-10: 1503380246

Publisher: AA Global Sourcing Ltd
Website: http://www.aaglobalsourcing.com

Table of Contents

Disclaimer 5
Dedication 6
Chapter 1: Introduction 7
Chapter 2: Lean Thinking in Government 11
Chapter 3: Eliminating Waste Using the Lean Process 15
Chapter 4: Doing More With Less 17
Chapter 5: Barriers to Lean's Success in Government 23
Chapter 6: Kaizen Blitz 27
Chapter 7: Lean Six Sigma 35
Chapter 8: Lean Six Sigma in Public Sector 45
Chapter 9: Designing a Public Sector that Absorbs the Variety of Customer Demand 51
Chapter 10: Strategies for Creating Lean Government 55
Chapter 11: Applying Lean to the Public Sector ... 65
Chapter 12: Lessons of Lean 79
Chapter 13: Why Every Government Should Embrace Lean 89
Chapter 14: Improving Value Creating Processes 93
Chapter 15: Pushing the Boundaries of Lean Management 101
Chapter 16: Lean Consumption at the Post Office 113
Chapter 17: Canada Post Lean Transformation . 115

Chapter 18: Lean Methodologies in Public Libraries 127
Chapter 19: The Lean Approach 133
Chapter 20: Lean Terminologies 137

Disclaimer

This publication is designed to provide competent and reliable information regarding the subject matter covered. However, it is sold with the understanding that the author and publisher are not engaged in rendering professional advice. The authors and publishers specifically disclaim any liability that is incurred from the use or application of contents of this book.

If you purchased this book without a cover you should be aware that this book may have been stolen property and reported as "unsold and destroyed" to the publisher. In this case neither the author nor the publisher has received any payment for this "stripped book."

Dedication

To my family and friends who seems to have been sent here to teach me something about who I am supposed to be. They have nurtured me, challenged me, and even opposed me…. But at every juncture has taught me!

This book is dedicated to my lovely boys, Thomas, Michael and Karl. Teaching them to manage their finance will give them the lives they deserve. They have taught me more about life, presence, and energy management than anything I have done in my life.

Chapter 1: Introduction

What is Lean?

A customer-driven waste reduction technique that:
1. Examines a current process.
2. Improves efficiency by decreasing process time.
3. Produces a product or service to the demand of internal and external customers.
4. Initiates organizational change.

Lean is the relentless pursuit of Waste. A Lean organization produces more with existing resources by eliminating non-value added activities. Lean establishes a systematic approach to eliminating these wastes and creating flow throughout the whole organization.

Lean Misconceptions

1. Lean is only for manufacturing businesses.
    a. Lean originated on the manufacturing shop floor, but was extended to service and support functions.
    b. Waste exists in all business processes.
    c. Eliminating waste improves stakeholder satisfaction.

2. Increasing productivity creates higher stress.
    a. Stress is higher when productivity is low and customer expectations are high.

3. Eliminating waste results in the loss of jobs.
   a. Frees up staff time to work on backlog of work.
   b. Can do new projects/do more for the customer.

4. Lean is a "Flavour of the Month".
   a. Lean is a sound, customer-centred business practice that results in improved outcomes.

5. Focusing on higher internal efficiency means less attention to the customer.
   a. Eliminating waste allows people to focus on customer satisfaction and new projects/opportunities.
   b. Documenting the process and making it transparent establishes the basis for customer value-added improvement.
   c. Frees up time to do more for the customer.

6. Lean costs a lot of money to implement.
   a. "Spend ideas, not money".
   b. People are greatly underutilized resources.

What is Waste?

Any step of a process that does not add value to the customer is considered Waste.

Examples of Waste:
1. Document errors.
2. Document transport.
3. Completing work not needed.
4. Process steps, reviews and approvals.

5. Waiting for the next step.
6. Searching for information.
7. Backlogs.
8. Behaviours.

Why Implement Lean?

Government is under increasing pressure to:
1. Reduce costs.
2. Expand services with less.
3. Improve processing time.
4. Increase productivity.
5. Improve quality of services.
6. Meet customer expectations.

How is it Done?

1. Obtain management commitment.
2. Identify a process/procedure to be "Leaned".
3. Establish a Lean team (include people who do the work).
4. Use Brainstorming/Process Mapping to identify "bottlenecks" and areas for improvement.
5. Implement customer-driven waste reduction techniques.
6. Evaluate the results and make further improvements.
7. Continue to find additional Lean projects within the unit.

So What is Lean Government?

Lean Government refers to the application of lean production (also known as "Lean") principles and methods to both identify and then implement the most efficient, value added way to provide government services. Government agencies have found that when Lean methods are implemented, they see an improved understanding of how their own processes work, that it facilitate the quick identification and implementation of improvements and that it builds a culture of continuous improvement.

Lean government proponents generally believe that the government should cut out "waste" and "inefficiency" from government organizations; this in turn will result in better services overall, as well as more value for tax-supported programs and services. Generally, proponents also see that a Lean government is a means to expand the capacity of government to provide more services per unit of investment.

5. Waiting for the next step.
6. Searching for information.
7. Backlogs.
8. Behaviours.

Why Implement Lean?

Government is under increasing pressure to:
1. Reduce costs.
2. Expand services with less.
3. Improve processing time.
4. Increase productivity.
5. Improve quality of services.
6. Meet customer expectations.

How is it Done?

1. Obtain management commitment.
2. Identify a process/procedure to be "Leaned".
3. Establish a Lean team (include people who do the work).
4. Use Brainstorming/Process Mapping to identify "bottlenecks" and areas for improvement.
5. Implement customer-driven waste reduction techniques.
6. Evaluate the results and make further improvements.
7. Continue to find additional Lean projects within the unit.

So What is Lean Government?

Lean Government refers to the application of lean production (also known as "Lean") principles and methods to both identify and then implement the most efficient, value added way to provide government services. Government agencies have found that when Lean methods are implemented, they see an improved understanding of how their own processes work, that it facilitate the quick identification and implementation of improvements and that it builds a culture of continuous improvement.

Lean government proponents generally believe that the government should cut out "waste" and "inefficiency" from government organizations; this in turn will result in better services overall, as well as more value for tax-supported programs and services. Generally, proponents also see that a Lean government is a means to expand the capacity of government to provide more services per unit of investment.

Chapter 2: Lean Thinking in Government

In these incredibly tough budget times, you would think government agencies would be working extra hard to find ways of doing things more efficiently. Unfortunately, leaders across the country are grabbing the same old playbook; recruitment freezes, travel restrictions, delaying maintenance and so on.

They are not examining the actual work being done; the operations are fundamentally the same. Instead, they are left with tired, overworked employees trying to do the same operations with fewer resources.

This approach creates an illusion of efficiency. Real efficiency is about looking at the systems; the way work itself is designed and finding ways to streamline the work so that we do our important tasks very well in less time and with less hassle. Systems are where the costs are incurred. Systems are where the customers show up. Systems are where the value of the agency is created and systems appear to be the last thing anyone is focusing on.

What exactly is Lean Government?

It's a mindset and a discipline to increase our capacity to do more good. There are four key steps:

1. Be clear about your purpose and bottom line. What good are you trying to create?

2. Know what customers want and what they value.

3. Build great widgets. Permits, child abuse investigation reports, substance abuse counselling programs, tax audits and so on.

4. Find a way to make the widgets better, faster and cheaper. Notice the sequence.

Lean is the reason Toyota dominates the auto market. Lean is the reason an Iowa business can get an environmental permit up to 90 percent faster these days. Lean is the reason Missouri taxpayers get their refunds in two days; all with fewer resources. Quite simply, Lean is the best hope for actually helping government deal with the challenge of crushing demand and limited resources.

So what make Lean so promising in government?

Three things.

1. Lean actually focuses on operations. The whole point of Lean is to rethink the way we produce what we produce, to increase our capacity to provide value to those we serve. Lean recognizes that inefficiency resides in our systems and our operations; the way we have designed our work. Lean is not another planning model, measurement method or accountability system. Lean is not a pithy slogan or something you tell employees to do. Lean actually focuses on the work of the agency.

2. Lean has a measurable impact on time, capacity and customer satisfaction. That is, it actually works. Lean projects produce amazing results, and they are often completed in as few as five days. The typical results of the teams I have worked with include 80 percent faster processes, 50 percents drops in customer waiting-times, doubling capacity, reducing phone calls and of course, savings costs.

How is this possible?

In United Kingdom we have a television series called "DIY SOS" On the show; the team will renovate a house in only seven days, as opposed to the nine to 12 months it typically takes builders to renovate similar house. How does the team do it? By focusing on all time-wasters and eliminating them. The team doesn't cut corners; the family still gets a roof; but the "Makeover" crew finds a way to work on the corners at the same time they are installing the plumbing.

That show is a perfect illustration of the opportunities in any process, government included. For almost any process, the actual labour accounts for less than 5 percent of the total time a process takes. So in a nine-month permitting process, there may be about two weeks of actual hard labour. A hiring process may involve three days of work stretched out over three to four months. Where does all that time go? Batching, bottlenecks, backlog, checking and re-checking. A Lean approach works to eradicate the lost time by eliminating these barriers. When the system runs faster, we can get more done with the same resources.

3. Lean involves employees. Specifically, the employees who work within the system being improved. We have tried employee involvement before, with suggestion programs, quality teams and so forth. While the intent of those programs was good, the focus was too small. Employees may be able to suggest ways to improve their own performance, or the piece of the process they are involved in. But systems cut across silos. Most employees can only see a part of the whole system; therefore, what might help them personally to be more productive could actually hinder the larger system. Lean projects, on the other hand, involve all the key players in a system (including the customers) to analyze the whole thing.

Lean has real promise. It has a chance to radically reshape government. The tenets of Lean are too important for this approach to be relegated to a mere fad. A fad is something we follow for a short time with exaggerated zeal. We desperately need "lean thinking" in government.

Chapter 3: Eliminating Waste Using the Lean Process

Lean process identifies the following seven wastes in service.

1. Defects/repairs/rejects/rework: Refers to poor quality due to method, design, process or material, e.g., errors in documents; drilling wrong size hole; improper patching of a pothole.

2. Transportation: Wasted effort in moving materials, e.g., transporting documents to several floors to get signatures; walking all the way across the plant to get parts.

3. Overproduction: Overproduction is a function of the mentality to produce more than necessary just to be on the safe side when one is worried about such problems as machine or equipment breakdowns, rejects, absenteeism, etc. All this results in using additional space for inventory or additional administrative costs, e.g., the order calls for making two tables, so you make three knowing that an additional one may be needed in a few weeks; two copies are requested but you make four just in case. In the lean process, overproduction is regarded as crime.

4. Waiting: Waiting occurs when one is waiting for the next step, waiting for parts, waiting for equipment to be repaired, waiting for someone to finish a document, waiting when someone puts you on hold, etc.

5. **Processing:** Inadequate technology or design leads to waste in the processing of work or service. Using the copy machine to sort and staple documents automatically, rather than performing those steps manually, helps reduce process time. Purchasing subassemblies can reduce the time wasted to assemble the parts. Eliminating a process not needed in the first place can reduce waste.

6. **Movement:** When a person is walking, he/she is not adding any value. Any action that requires great physical exertion should be avoided or eliminated. Rearranging a workplace can eliminate unnecessary walking. Not having a well-organized and well-maintained work area leads to wasted time and motion in locating the parts or items needed for the process.

7. **Inventory:** When excessive parts, supplies, semi-finished products or final products are kept on hand, they add to the cost of operation or service by occupying space, requiring additional facilities and unnecessary administration to maintain the inventory.

Anything that does not add value is waste and therefore this list can be extended to represent the process or the service. In addition, improper use of talent is considered a waste. Employing certain professionals to jobs that can be mechanized or assigned to less skilled people is considered a waste of talent.

Chapter 4: Doing More With Less

There is no doubt that the public sector is in an extremely challenging environment, with both central and local government faced with the task of maintaining public services against a back drop of smaller budgets and lower tax receipts and income. There is increasing demand in some areas, higher social security payments, and the knock on effects of declines in key sectors such as financial services and construction. The public continue to demand greater service and with less money available, no organisation has the luxury of being wasteful.

Seeking greater efficiencies is of course not a new idea. Progress has certainly been made and there are many examples in the public sector which illustrate this. In addition the gradual use of Lean Thinking (or Systems Thinking as it is sometimes referred to) has helped many organisations achieve improvements and reduce costs; however we are not convinced that some of the initiatives and savings sought for the public sector will deliver the significant long term and sustained performance that the Treasury needs to help it progress towards a more balanced budget. That is why we believe it's time for all public sector organisations to investigate how the application of Lean thinking could help them in transforming the economics of their service delivery.

Used properly, Lean can help public sector organisations to maintain high standard of services, despite the cuts. The call has been to do 'more with less' in other words, to be more efficient. But care must be taken to ensure that the focus is not solely on taking the money out this to a degree is the easy bit. There are, in fact, two ways in which to increase value; one, by reducing waste and thus the cost of a product or service; the other, by increasing value adding activities. The challenge for public sector organisations is to reduce spend whilst retaining or even improving service delivery. The call therefore is 'better with less'.

This chapter aims to demystify the term Lean and explain how this approach can deliver better services at lower cost for the public sector. The benefits that can be achieved include.

1. Effective management decisions due to heavy reliance on data and facts instead of gut. Feelings and hunches. Hence costs associated with fire fighting and misdirected problem solving efforts with no structured or disciplined methodology could be significantly reduced.

2. Increased understanding of customer needs and expectations, especially the critical-to-quality (CTQ) service performance characteristics which will have the greatest impact on customer satisfaction and loyalty.

3. More efficient and reliable processes.

4. Improved knowledge across the organisation on various tools and techniques for problem solving, leading to greater job satisfaction for employees.

5. Reduced number of non-value-added operations through systematic elimination, leading to faster delivery of service, faster lead time, faster cycle time to process critical performance characteristics to customers and stakeholders, etc.

6. Reduced variability in process performance, service capability, reliability, delivery and performance, leading to more predictable and consistent level of quality and service performance.

7. Transformation of organisational culture from being reactive to proactive thinking / mind-set.

So for public sector organisations, the benefits are clear; sustainable cost reductions in the delivery of services, while still delivering quality and value to the users of the service.

The Key Lean Thinking Principles

In 'Lean Thinking' (Womack and Jones, 1996) five Lean principles were put forward as a framework to be used by an organisation to implement Lean Thinking. A key initial premise is to recognise that only a small fraction of the total time and effort when producing a product or delivering a service actually adds value for the end customer. It is therefore critical to clearly define value for a specific product or service from the end customer's perspective, so that all the non-value activities or waste can be targeted for removal step by step.

Womack and Jones' five principles are.
1. Specify what creates value from the customers perspective.
2. Identify all steps across the whole value stream.
3. Make those actions that create value flow.
4. Only make what is pulled by the customer just-in-time.
5. Strive for perfection by continually removing successive layers of waste.

Few services are provided by one function alone, so that waste removal has to be pursued throughout the whole 'value stream' the entire set of activities across all the entities involved in jointly delivering the service. New relationships are required to eliminate waste and to effectively manage the value stream as a whole. Instead of managing the workload through successive departments, processes need to flow through all the value adding steps without interruption, using the toolbox of Lean techniques to successively remove the obstacles to flow to meet the demand from the end customer.

Removing wasted time and effort represents the biggest opportunity for performance improvement and enabling a greater focus on creating value.

Lean places greater emphasis on wasteful activity and in line with this, Toyota identified seven deadly wastes related to activity rather than design and implementation; transportation issues, inventory control issues, unnecessary movement of persons or equipment, time management, overproducing concerns, over-processing, and errors. Significant costs may be attached to each of these types of waste. As more and more layers of waste become visible and the process continues every action needs to add value for the end customer.

In this way, Lean Thinking represents a path of sustained performance improvement and not a one off programme.

As Lean Thinking contends services must think strategically beyond its own boundaries. Because value streams flow across several departments and functions within an organisation, it needs to be organised around its key value streams. This includes enhancing the value delivered by internal service and back office operations ... Finance, Human Resources, Legal and Compliance, Customer Service, Information Technology, Marketing, Facilities Management, etc.

Lean Thinking principles can be applied to any organisation in any sector. Although lean's origins are largely from an automotive manufacturing environment, the principles and techniques are been transferred to many sectors, often with little adaptation. Despite scepticism by many that techniques and philosophies designed in a manufacturing context apply elsewhere, sectors such as distribution, housing, construction, healthcare, financial services, and other public sector services have all begun to implement Lean ideas in recent years.

Irrespective of the sector you work in, Lean is rooted in two key principles; "continuous improvement" and "respect for people". The "continuous improvement" principle embodies the tools and methods used to improve productivity and reduce costs. The "respect for people" principle embodies leadership behaviours and business practices that must be consistent with efforts to eliminate waste and create value for end use customers.

Chapter 5: Barriers to Lean's Success in Government

1. The industrial jargon is a turn-off. Having lived through TQM and reengineering in government, I saw first-hand how repulsed public-sector people get with private-sector terminology. Visions of "ISO-9000 certified factories producing just-in-time defect-free widgets" did not light a fire under government managers. The Lean terminology of waste, value stream, Toyota Production System, supply-chain, and 5S isn't helping either. All of these terms conjure up visions of cogs in a machine mass-producing undifferentiated widgets for happy customers. This is the exact opposite of how most people view their work in government.

The Lean concepts of increasing capacity, making processes flow more smoothly and understanding what customers value; can have a huge impact on government performance but only if people in government believe the concepts apply to them. The more we obfuscate helpful concepts with industrial-age terminology, the more barriers we put up to achieving change.

2. Government executives generally don't care about operations. Most elected officials and government executives didn't join government to manage. Instead, they are driven by a deep desire to advance a cause, a policy issue or a political agenda. They get excited about bold new programs and solving big problems

not about making the widgets. But the key to results in government is a combination of innovative policy and improving the performance of operations. There has to be a balance between "bold new stuff" and improving the "stuff we already have." Right now, though, the balance is out of whack. We have too much emphasis on policies, programs, politics and people and not emphasis on our processes. So how do you get government executives and policy makers to care about operations? That brings us to barrier number three.

3. The emphasis of Lean is on the wrong thing. The current focus of Lean is on reducing waste. This is a noble intention, of course. But I fear that, unless the Lean practitioners rethink their message, they will meet the same fate as Total Quality Management. TQM struggled in government for two key reasons; first, the manufacturing jargon; and second, TQM was ultimately an elaborate solution to a problem we weren't having. The emphasis of TQM was to reduce defects and it did an amazing job at it. The control charts, the histograms, the fish-bone diagrams all helped identify, measure and reduce defects. So why didn't government jump on the bandwagon? Why weren't there Pareto charts in every agency lobby? Because reducing defects was not the problem in government. Government biggest hurdle doesn't involve defects or mistakes. The number-one challenge facing government is capacity. Simply, they don't have enough resources to keep up with ever-expanding and ever-more complex workloads.

That is why I am really excited about the promise of Lean for government. I have seen first-hand that this approach gets to the heart of improving government: It increases government capacity to do more good and that is how we address barrier number two, how we get executives to start caring about operations. When we improve the processes of government, we free up the capacity to take on the "bold new stuff." That is what Lean should be emphasizing not the waste-reduction itself, but the ultimate effect that has, allowing managers to tackle the items on their wish lists.

There is a belief that when the current economic crisis lifts, we will all go back to life as normal. I am not that optimistic. People in government have not met this crisis by fundamentally rethinking what they do and how they do it. They have met the fiscal challenges by cutting positions and freezing spending; they will come out of the crisis with less capacity to accomplish government services than they had before.

That is why the aftermath of this economics crisis is the perfect time to use the principles of Lean to radically rethink what we do and how we do it. We should use this time to help policy makers understand the potential of improving the operations of government. Will it succeed? If we can overcome our limiting beliefs, get past the language barrier and tap into people's desire to make a difference, then we have got a real chance.

Chapter 6: Kaizen Blitz

Imagine you wake up one morning realising you have a sore head, the usual remedies don't work, you think it may even be something quite serious, you take a trip to the Doctor's, then imagine your surprise when the Doctor asks you no questions but suggests the real problem is your leg, even worse the remedy is simply more aspirin, wouldn't you be concerned? I am sure this situation never occurs in a Doctor's surgery but in some local councils in the United Kingdom improper diagnosis and prescription error are soon to be the way of dealing with organisational ills and the new medicine; Kaizen Blitz.

Kaizen Blitz seems like a rational way to go about change. Get the managers to define a problem, label all the parts of the process that seem wasteful, brainstorm ideas for the removal of said waste, and instantly implement the change to those who work in the operations (including many individuals that were not privy to the project and its goals). Supporters of the method claim that it gives people an idea how much change can be created in a short period of time (a day or so), thus creating an appetite for continuous improvement through the whole organisation and don't get me wrong I am not a naysayer to improving our public services; it is long overdue but the problem is method. Critics of Kaizen Blitz, and I am among them, argue that not only does it fail to reach the right diagnosis about the nature of the problem but that its method of fixing problems is also flawed.

Fans say that Kaizen Blitz is analogous to 'lean', it isn't. Lean works on the basis of first understanding value from a customers' point of view and then analyzing the system responsible for the creation of that value end-to-end. The goal in a lean intervention is to reduce the waste involved in providing value for the customer; the means is changing the system, as Toyota showed in manufacturing. In service, whilst the principles are the same, the practicalities differ considerably. The first requirement is to understand demand, the type and frequency of demand into a system or service. Further, equal amounts of waste in service organisations are found not just in the process but in having to deal with the fall-out from its failure. To date our work has shown that most public sector demand is failure demand e.g. "why haven't you called yet, it's been done wrong etc" the greatest leverage therefore is to reduce the 50-60% of demand that consumes most resource and money. Both lean in manufacturing and in service state that processes should be studied end to end from the customers' point of view; this is not a feature of Kaizen Blitz.

Kaizen Blitz is borne out of the command and control school of management. Here the doctrine is that management knows best about the work and how it should be done; it's their belief that only management can design policies and procedures for doing the work; and should staff get sick of this regime then targets and service standards will sort them out and remind them why their job is so damned attractive. Command and control helped Henry Ford move from craft work to mass production, and he was first to institute the five dollar day, unfortunately he is also credited with the five day man; conditions in his plants being so bad, i.e. boring and repetitive, that even on high wages the Ford man stayed for only five days.

Kaizen Blitz is pretend 'lean', done command and control style. Management define what processes (more often parts of processes) should be tackled and most commonly map these processes in a room. Then having decided on the problem, the process is redesigned with all the old service standards and targets (part of the problem) still in place. It's why command and control managers love it, they can give the impression of changing things without actually changing things, and the message to the staff is "see, you were doing it wrong, and we fixed it for you" and some say not only are its design principles wrong but that it simply doesn't work, often failing to address the root of the problem.

Kaizen Blitz: Though the areas selected for rapid improvement can often show gains they hardly ever address the right problem or system constraint. Kaizen Blitz just pushes the problem around the plant never getting the source of the issue and upsetting most people who come to work to do a good job.

Kaizen Blitz's failure to identify organisational constraints and the use of 'outsiders' who impose change, based on limited data collection, on those who do the work. Though it seems like fast gains are achieved the real problem is never tackled especially when Kaizen Blitz is applied to a non-bottleneck or constraint. Sure large gains are possible on non critical process points in a chain but for manufacturers you won't get any more saleable product out and for service businesses you will just play a game of command, impose and control; so much for the latent intellectual capital of workers! Kaizen Blitz is just a mirage for most businesses and worse it lowers the credibility of management.

In service organisations the problem is exacerbated as the constraint is not usually a lack capacity but in the work design or the behaviour of front line staff as driven by management measures or policy. For example if you studied housing repairs you would see that most of the waste is associated with jobs constantly being opened and closed in order to meet management targets; in council owned sports centres you discover booking a room means the completion of multiple (wasteful) forms. Kaizen Blitz will not address the real causes of waste in the public sector; the source of the problems is usually linked to the measures, functions or job role designs. The big problem with Kaizen Blitz is that it is not systemic and therefore assumes that all problems are localised and can be solved simply by process re-engineering; what a great way of avoiding the real problem and remaining internally focused.

Other key factors in the evaluation of change methods should be their sustainability and how front line staff are involved. Kaizen Blitz is not appropriate for looking at complex systems involving many functions or departments. It is not suitable when the problem area is not well-defined or when the unsatisfactory performance of the current state is due to many factors that inter-connect and vary over time, meaning that the conditions prevailing for study at the time of the event may be unrepresentative. The intensive nature of Kaizen Blitz means that the team are on a deadline to implement change by the end of the week. Where Kaizen Blitz is applied inappropriately, the actions implemented usually tackle symptoms and not causes; because the system is unchanged there is no permanent improvement in performance. This is damaging to the motivation and self-esteem of those employees who took part in the event and reduces the engagement in future change activities.

Council services are complex systems, the behaviour of which is determined by management policy and measures. To date I have never heard of a Kaizen Blitz event that tackled these issues; it is therefore unlikely to be sustainable. Further, though in some cases staff are involved in the redesign of the chosen area they do this without proper understanding of the problem as this has been defined by management. In Japan Kaizen Blitz is seen as an abhorrent method; its activities are a way to humiliate managers and company employees that have provided consistently poor performance. In Europe, and the UK in particular, research shows local team leaders and front line staff are rarely involved and they quickly put the system back to the way they were as there is no buy-in. For one automotive component manufacturer this was as quick as the evening of the blitz event itself.

So far I have criticised managers for failing to understand the difference between Kaizen Blitz and lean, and further criticism is levelled at Kaizen Blitz as it is a poor method for change. But is there anything positive to be said about Kaizen Blitz?

To use Kaizen Blitz effectively, a clear design of the desired future state of the system is needed. This can only come from an analysis of the current system and an understanding through data of the causes of failure to perform to achieve the required outcome. Second, a detailed action plan of the changes needed to make the transformation from current to future system. Some of these actions may lend themselves to application of the Kaizen Blitz approach but many will not and will require other styles of intervention and implementation methods. Third, the leadership of the organisation needs to communicate the future state and state their support for changes in policy and systems in order to engage the employees in taking part in developing the new ways of working needed. If you have all these in place, then you have the foundations for the successful implementation of change. Kaizen Blitz may have a part to play in the implementation of change; it is not the right tool for analysing what to change or designing what to change to. My main point is that whilst it (Kaizen Blitz) may have part to play in the implementation it is useless as a tool for analysis.

Kaizen blitz is misused by organisations who want a quick fix to deep rooted-problems. If there were a quick fix to the problems in the public sector would we not have found it by now? More of the same is not the answer. Is it not time to try to properly address the problems caused by bad management in the public sector? Our councils are sick, they have a disease called command and control. The problem is systemic and must be removed at the root, this means inoculating all managers with a new way of thinking or simply removing those that cannot be cured. Unfortunately ministers don't seem to have the stomach to do either, so expect more bad service at high cost and for the managers two aspirins and some low hanging fruit should be in order.

Chapter 7: Lean Six Sigma

Six Sigma is a process improvement methodology that has been proven to make step function improvement in any business environment. Six Sigma is driven by quality. It uses facts and data focused on customer value. It is not a one-time project to fix a problem. It is not a "Flash in the Pan" or a "Flavour of the month" program that will go away. Six Sigma is a structured way to approach your business issues. If Six Sigma is embraced and implemented into your organisation's culture you can achieve about a 20% margin improvement, 15% capacity improvement and/or a 20% capital reduction. Six Sigma defines customer value as a product or service that is received by a customer at the right;
1. Location
2. Cost
3. Time
4. Delivers

All of these as defined by the customer, not you. Many time we see customer value as the "functions" part only that the product worked or the service did what it was supposed to do. But we forget that customer value includes the delivery process that is made up of the other three items above; location, cost, and point in time.

In the 1980s, engineers at Motorola Corporation developed Six Sigma as a business improvement methodology. They discovered the mathematically derived point where the cost of eliminating an error/defect is greater than the cost of living with (and repairing) the defect. That is, there is an acceptable point of imperfection and any quality improvement made beyond that point is more expensive than the expected cost savings of fixing the imperfection.

Motorola explained that Six Sigma (which represents 3.4 defects per million) is the optimum level to balance quality and cost. This discovery forced Motorola to assess quality levels by measuring defects in millions rather than thousands, which had been the traditional method. This change enabled a vast improvement in the ability to assess and improve quality levels. Six Sigma enabled Motorola to cost efficiently perform defect free more than 90% of the time, resulting in significant savings. Its objective is to find and eliminate causes of defects or mistakes in processes by focusing on outputs. Even a Sigma level of 6 though gives.
1. 500 surgical operations failed per week.
2. 1000 letters lost per hour.
3. Every day 15,000 cheques charged to a wrong account.

So every process has the potential for error, and the idea is to look at all the ways in which things can go wrong, especially in the eyes of the customer, and try and eliminate the defects.

Take for example the business of a planning application to a Local Authority. The process begins with your first call to the planning department. Various things can go wrong: you can be placed in a queue and have an unacceptably long wait, you can be passed between departments, or when you receive the document you notice that your details have been recorded incorrectly or that you are being charged a higher amount than you were quoted in the phone call.

Six Sigma also looks at "excessive variation in processes" for example, the same x-ray on the same machine with the same operator may take 15 minutes one day and 21 minutes the next. Why? How can we reduce this variation?

Six Sigma Principles.

1. Understand the critical to quality requirements (CTQs) of our customers and stakeholders.

2. Understand our processes ensuring they reflect these CTQs.

3. Manage by fact:
   a. Measurement and management by fact enables more effective decision making.
   b. By understanding variation we will also know when to take action and when not to.

4. Involve and equip the people in the process.

5. Undertake improvement activity in a systematic way.

Six Sigma Today

While the concept of Six Sigma began in the manufacturing arena decades ago, the idea that organisations can improve quality levels and work "defect free" is currently being used by public sector organisation of all types and sizes.

Naturally, as Six Sigma permeates into today's complex, sophisticated government landscape, the methodology is "tweaked" to satisfy unique needs of individual public bodies. But no matter how it is deployed, there is an overall framework that drives Six Sigma toward improving government performance.

Common Six Sigma traits include.

1. A process of improving quality by gathering data, understanding and controlling variation, and improving predictability of the organisation's business processes.

2. A formalised Define, Measure, Analyse, Improve, Control (DMAIC) process that is the blueprint for Six Sigma improvements. (The DMAIC process will be described in greater detail later in this chapter.)

3. A strong emphasis on value. Six Sigma projects focus on high return areas where the greatest benefits can be gained.

4. Internal cultural change, beginning with support from leaders and champions.

By defining, measuring, and analysing a business's processes, Six Sigma is able to improve the effectiveness of its operations as well as to design services of a quality that is likely to suit the needs of potential customers. More importantly, not addressing the quality issues can in time result in less efficient processes.

Based on Facts and Data

Six Sigma uses facts and data to understand, reduce and control variation in your business processes, variation that you now compensate for which costs you money. This is not about analysing reports which you may receive on a weekly or monthly basis. Go and see what is happening out in the workplace and collect real data on how things are done. One local authority Chief Executive would listen to contact centre recordings to understand what was actually taking place.

It is the difference between what you think is happening and what is really happening. There is variation everywhere. To reduce it or eliminate it you first have to understand it. Understanding and addressing variation helps you predict outcomes that you had to compensate for before; outcomes that impact your customer needs. In Six Sigma these facts and data on the variation are collected and analysed to come up with conclusions which lead to better decisions.

Lean Six Sigma Bringing them Together

Operating by itself, Lean focuses on using the minimum amount of resources (people, materials, and capital) to produce solutions and deliver them on time to customers. Lean implementation can involve extremely thorough data collection and analysis that take years before any change occurs. This approach often yields desired results, but takes too long to get there.

Meanwhile, Six Sigma, operating independently, aims to improve quality by enhancing knowledge generating processes. In many cases, this leads to slow, deliberate, change intolerant practices. To combat these challenges, organisations have found that by merging the Lean methodology with the Six Sigma methodology, a synergy is achieved that provides results much greater than if each of the approaches was implemented individually.

When Lean is added to Six Sigma, slow processes are challenged and replaced with more streamlined workflows. Additionally, the data gathered during Lean implementation helps identify the highest impact Six Sigma opportunities. When Six Sigma is added to Lean, a much needed structure is provided that makes it easier to consistently and predictably achieve optimum flow. The two methodologies work so well together, that a new, integrated, Lean Six Sigma approach, with its own unique characteristics, has been defined and incorporated by several leading organisations.

Lean Six Sigma therefore is the application of Lean techniques to increase speed and reduce waste, while employing Six Sigma processes to improve quality and focus on the Voice of the Customer. Lean Six Sigma means doing things right the first time, only doing the things that generate value, and doing it all quickly and efficiently. When meshed together as Lean Six Sigma, each of these ideals serves to increase delivery speed while decreasing variation in performance. As a result, Lean Six Sigma allows managers to effectively address issues of speed, quality, and cost.

The Lean Six Sigma based on DMAIC approach.

With this methodology, a team defines a problem and works through to implementing a solution linked to its underlying causes, establishing practices to ensure the solution sticks.

1. Define

The Define phase of the DMAIC process is often skipped or short changed, but is vital to the overall success of any Lean Six Sigma project. This is the phase where the current state, problem statement, and desired future state are determined and documented via the Project Charter.

2. Measure

The Measure phase is where the business gathers quantitative and qualitative data to get a clear view of the current state. This serves as a baseline to evaluate potential solutions and typically involves interviews with process owners, process mapping of the key business processes, and gathering data relating to current performance (time, volume, frequency, impact, etc.). Information that gives a clear view of the current state is found in numerous locations and all of it is valuable and should be captured.

3. Analyse

In the Analyse phase, the business studies the information gathered in the Measure phase, pinpoints bottlenecks, and identifies improvement opportunities where non-value-add tasks can be removed. A business case is conducted, which takes into account not only hard costs but also intangible benefits that can be gained, such as productivity and satisfaction, to determine if the improvement is cost effective and worthwhile.

4. Improve

The Improve phase is when recommended solutions are implemented. A project plan is developed and put into action, beginning with a pilot programme and culminating in full scale deployment. Where appropriate, new technology is implemented, workflows are streamlined, and unnecessary processes are eliminated. Key factors of success during this phase are acceptance by end users and change without any degradation of current productivity levels.

5. Control

The Control phase is where the business ensures the solution consistently delivers.

So why do it?

Lean Six Sigma's goal is growth, not just reducing costs. Its aim is effectiveness, not just efficiency. In this way, a Lean Six Sigma approach drives organisations not just to do things better but to do better things. In the past, companies used Lean Six Sigma primarily for operational improvement; refining existing processes to reduce costs, improve performance and provide better customer value; however, dramatic upheavals in the competitive marketplace are prompting business change on a more significant scale. Organisations must innovate, not just improve.

Despite its heritage, Lean Six Sigma is well suited for this step change in target and scope. Because of its core tenets analysis based on facts and direct customer input. Lean Six Sigma is equipped to facilitate a much broader transformation, helping an organisation rethink its entire business and create a more innovative climate.

Chapter 8: Lean Six Sigma in Public Sector

How can Lean Six Sigma help government cut costs and still deliver a better level of service?

One of the reasons it has only been recently applied is that, unlike manufacturing, it is very hard to see a physical product in services and follow it through its key processing from raw material to finished product. In the service world the service product is hidden within many interconnected departments. This is why it can take weeks to complete a simple service because of invisible hand offs, bottlenecks and non-ownership of the process as it crosses inter-department fiefdoms all with their own measurements for performance.

Many managers lack statistical knowledge and the ability to apply statistics to problem solving. If you look at management development programmes, how many devote time within their programmes to practical and applied statistical methods. So the challenge is to motivate the managers to understand and apply statistical methods. It is a fundamental framework for managers to use these techniques for problem solving in organisations.

There is a real gap. One of the problems is short-term thinking by senior managers. We need to change the mind-set which thinks just for short-term results and which lacks a clear vision or strategic direction. We need to move away from creating fire-fighting managers who only tackle problems that arise on a daily basis without determining the root cause, so the problems come back again and again. There is a big need for a change in culture. We need brave leaders setting direction and looking at how we transform businesses.

Lean Six Sigma brings powerful methods for quickly combating recessionary pressures, and its application in the service sector and office environment unlocks significant opportunities to reduce costs, remove waste and improve the overall customer experience. It provides a compelling option for consideration, not least because it helps organisations across the public and private sector to achieve cost reductions without sacrificing service quality.

Improvement activity must be tailored to circumstances if benefits are to be sustained and in reality, different approaches are often brought together to deliver the right result. 'Lean Six Sigma' recognises that the improvement strengths of Lean can be harnessed with the financial benefits and analytical discipline of Six Sigma to create benefits on a far greater scale.

It is a systematic method to improve an organisation's capability to meet customer demands, and identifies ways to deliver improved customer service at lower cost; in other words: "achieving much better with less".

By putting Lean six Sigma principles into practice, we believe public sector organisations can offer high performing services that typically achieve.

1. A clear focus on the issues that matter most to customers and other stakeholders.

2. An understanding of customer demand and how this can vary.

3. Greater responsiveness and flexibility to meet customer needs.

4. More effective service delivery, at reduced cost.

5. Whole systems' improvement through more capable end-to-end processes.

So Why Do Politicians Ignore It?

United State of America Department of Defence, thousands of private sector companies and even the state government of Iowa uses it, so why are Congress and the president silent on it?

Six Sigma, and more specifically Lean Six Sigma (LSS), has made a resurgence into the national political dialogue in recent years in tandem with surging government inefficiency and perennial $1.5 trillion federal deficits. Top lawmakers would be wise to take note and lead on this topic.

Lean Six Sigma is a process that was first used by Motorola and then popularized by General Electric

CEO Jack Welch in the mid 1990's that determines waste and inefficiencies within supply chains and organization processes. By using Lean Six Sigma, companies have saved hundreds of billions over the past two decades. GE's success in using it proved that it paid off. Other companies that have also used Lean Six Sigma to improve efficiency and save money are 3M, ACME, Sears, Dell, DuPont Whirlpool, Xerox, and many more.

Former U.S. Representative and former Speaker of the House Newt Gingrich made Lean Six Sigma (LSS) one of his core campaign platforms. National political advocacy groups like Strong America Now and Gingrich's own Lean Six Sigma coalition, Effective Government Now, were full of thousands of Lean Six professionals discussing ways to cut waste in government on a daily basis.

Following the economic downturn of 2007 and 2008 the efficiency of government has come under more scrutiny than ever before as U.S. national deficit continually surpasses $1 trillion a year. Much of the anger directed at the federal government has come from the small business community that sees government acting in a fashion that would drive any private enterprise into bankruptcy. While the private sector is tightening its belt and learning to live with a myriad of new regulations and taxes, the federal government still refuses to seriously address entitlement program insolvency and thousands of redundancies across all government departments.

Out of this debate have emerged many calls for the government to adopt the same Six Sigma type of radical management change that General Electric and other companies utilized 20-30 years ago.

On May 15th 2008, U.S. Deputy Defence Secretary Gordon England took the unconventional step of ordering all Defence Department components to adopt Lean Six Sigma.

That certainly does not sound like a politician; but it should in these days of layered analytics and reporting.

The Department of Defence is trying to duplicate the outstanding results seen by the U.S. Army and Navy implementations of Lean Six Sigma in 2005 and 2006 when they saved a combined $2.45 billion as of 2008; however it isn't just the U.S. military that is adopting Lean Six Sigma. The Iowa Department of Management adopted Lean Six Sigma in 2003. The state saw dramatic results across the board including a 50% reduction in most process lead times in the Department of Natural Resources.

The success of Lean Six Sigma in the private sector and select government agencies proves the system is effective. Yet Congress and the president's lack of regard for adopting it across the board, despite its success, is both troubling and unsurprising.

If USA and counties worldwide are going to get serious about addressing their largest national security threat; "debt" they must get as equally serious about reform. The best course of action is to look at what is working in the private sector and in other areas of government.

Lean Six Sigma is a serious solution for serious problems. It is time we hear more politicians talking about it.

Chapter 9: Designing a Public Sector that Absorbs the Variety of Customer Demand

Lean is a wicked disease and public sectors are waking up to the problem.

I am increasingly being asked for advice by leaders of service organisations who are anxious about their 'lean' programme. Their most frequent concern is that the 'improvements' detailed in copious project reports are not reflected in the bottom line; claimed savings adding up to a sizeable fraction of total costs simply refuse to appear.

I ask them first of all how they manage their service operations. Have they divided the work between specialised front and back-offices, and do they manage it with work-flow methods? Do they manage the activity of their workers, and are they using standard times? Do they invest in people management programmes? I know that, most often, the answers to all these questions will be 'yes'.

Then I ask if the lean projects have been targeted at management's current problems. Do managers determine the problems the lean projects must tackle? And I ask for examples of problems the projects are set up to 'improve'. Many are to do with reducing activity times; the second most popular are aimed at standardising the work.

When I enquire where the word 'lean' came from, a few will know that it was coined by an American to describe Toyota's famous production system. Fewer are aware that the TPS was developed by Taiichi Ohno, and fewer still that its author was strongly opposed to codifying the methods and even writing them down at all.

Ohno argued that codifying the TPS would ossify into a trivial set of tools something that had emerged through trial and error from a different way of thinking. I tell them how Ohno taught his managers, by having them study the work; the direct reverse of the all-too-common assumption that improvement begins with the application of tools to problems whose nature is already known..

Then I ask how many people in the room are making cars at the rate of customer demand and if not (after all these are service organisations), why would they assume that the tools developed for this specific purpose would solve the problems of delivering services?

Why did Ohno teach his managers by getting them to study the system? Because only careful study of the work reveals what the true problems are and mostly they are not the ones you thought they were. In fact, this revelation is frequently followed by an even more challenging one; the real issue is actually the way you were thinking about your problems and so it is with service organisations. Managers assume that standardising work cuts costs, yet when they study their services they find that standard processes prevent the system from absorbing variety; in simple terms, it makes it hard for customers to get what they want, and the organisation consumes more resources as a consequence. It is a hard lesson. The reality that standardisation drives costs up will be resisted, rationalised and angrily denied. This is why managers have to be there, studying the work; only when they see the evidence with their own eyes does acceptance become energy channelled into constructive change.

Studying the work reveals other counterintuitive truths. The harmful consequence of managing activity as cost is a second prime example. The specialisation and standardisation of work, both resulting in lower transaction costs, also lead to more handovers, fragmentation of the work, duplication and re-work that more than cancel out any gain. Service managers learn the paradox that managing costs creates costs, something Ohno discovered to be true in manufacturing.

The truth is that lean tools interventions reinforce rather than challenge management's assumptions. The opportunity to standardise work and reduce activity times is warmly welcomed by managers who have grown up in modern industrialised service organisations. Beguiled by the plausible notion that improvement tools are universal, managers have introduced a wicked disease that instead of curing worsens the condition of the patient by amplifying inherent weaknesses.

As benefits refuse to materialise and symptoms gets worse, the dysfunction becomes apparent to leaders with enquiring minds. They realise that their problems lie in industrialised processes, as they did for Ohno, and how re-thinking industrialised processes enables them to design better services at much lower cost, as Ohno did with cars and they learn that while Ohno was developing a system for producing cars at the rate of customer demand, the problem they need to solve is designing a service organisation that absorbs the variety of customer demand, in real time. When they do, they realise profound benefits, as Ohno did before them.

Chapter 10: Strategies for Creating Lean Government

Lean government. The very idea sounds implausible. Even to the seasoned Lean practitioner, the idea of a Lean government sounds farfetched. Governments are traditionally seen as the epitome of bureaucracy and the guardians of red tape, incomprehensible forms and endless queues. But there are workable Lean strategies for governments seeking to reduce waste and become more efficient. Eight are outlined here. Perhaps considering the eight ideas can spur government change agents to study Lean literature for potential improvement applications and in the longer run, start a Lean revolution in governments.

One-piece Flow

Consider 10 firemen passing a bucket of water from one to the next and ultimately to the fire. One-piece flow is achieved when the time it takes to pass a bucket from one fireman to the next is always exactly the same. If just one fireman is out of synch, the bucket flow will be disrupted and the entire chain will slow down.

The idealized goal of Lean is "one-piece flow," also known as continuous flow. One-piece flow is achieved when all waste is eliminated from the value stream and all that remains is value-added work from the perspective of customers. In manufacturing, one-piece flow is an ideal and will always be an ideal because of fluctuations in customer demands plus the customer requirements for ever shorter delivery time forces the manufacturer to create partially completed or completed inventories. This type of manufacturing strategy actually creates waste because there is a need for storage and management of storage.

The interesting thing about Lean in government is that one-piece flow operation is almost achievable here because there is really no requirement for in-process inventories. There is really no such thing as a partially finished job that is not the result of a customer order within government processes.

What would one-piece flow feel like in a typical government value stream?

Most governments and their value streams are not lean. Recall personal experiences trying to obtain a government grant, applying for an international passport, getting a drivers license or applying for a business permit. The typical experience is that is not that it took just three hours. More likely, it took more than a week. Nonetheless, it is possible to make government value streams lean. Here are eight ways:

1. Synchronization to Customer Demands

Most government value streams are not designed and synchronized to customer demands. In Lean manufacturing, the concept of Takt time, or beat time, is well understood but within most governments, this concept is unheard of. Takt time is a concept that is used to design work and it measures the pace of customer demand. It is the "available time for production" divided by the "customer demand." The resulting number tells how fast each process step must operate to obtain one-piece flow.

Here is a government example. Suppose 300 citizens apply for a particular government permit in one working day and each working day consists of six working hours. The Takt time of this permit application process is 360 (6 x 60) minutes divided by 300 applications, which is equal to 1.2 minutes. This means that for these 300 applications to be processed within that one working day, every 1.2 minutes, one permit must processed to satisfy the customer demand.

The first permit will take the sum of all processing times to complete. Suppose there are 10 processing steps, each synchronized to Takt at 1.2 minutes each; then the first permit will take 12 minutes to complete. If one-piece flow is achieved, the next permit in the queue will leave the line exactly 1.2 minutes after the first permit and so on. To complete all 300 permits, it will actually take 12 minutes plus (299 x 1.2) totalling 371 minutes, assuming one-piece flow operations.

To achieve this, the cycle time for each processing step must be 1.2 minutes or less to meet the demand. If any processing step takes more than 1.2 minutes, it becomes a bottleneck and work will get stuck at that point.

Government value streams are rarely designed around Takt time because the concept does not exist within most governments. Most public sector administrators do not understand how such a concept can translate into their environment. As a result, workforce allocations in government value streams are rarely rationalized around Takt time, resulting in over capacity in some parts of the stream and under capacity in other parts.

The main waste that this produces is work-in-process inventory (WIP) and the most visible manifestation of this is the ever-full in-tray. Work-in-process kills one-piece flow because it disables a processing step from producing to Takt. But Work-in-process build up is inevitable in any government value stream that is not synchronized to Takt. This is the main reason why a three-hour job needs more than a week for processing.

2. Understand Variations in Customer Demand

Synchronization to Takt generally requires two things; reducing the processing time of the step and establishing the correct staffing level. Suppose it takes six minutes to complete the application process at the government counter. To achieve one-piece flow at a Takt time of 1.2 minutes (as in the previous example) would require the manning of at least five counters (6 divided by 1.2 minutes). This assumes that one customer arrives into the stream every 1.2 minutes. Reducing the processing time to three minutes would allow the manning level to be reduced to three counters (3 divided by 1.2 minutes).

Of course, customers do not normally arrive at specific intervals. Most value streams experience significant variation in customer demand throughout the course of any typical workday. When the counter process is not synchronized to fluctuating customer demand, the familiar queue builds up. The typical government response to this problem is to build waiting areas and queue ticketing systems. This wastes not only expensive floor space (which taxpayers pay for) but more importantly it wastes the time of the citizens (customers). In some of the government value streams, this queuing can take up to hours.

This happens because fluctuations in customer demands typically are not monitored and also because government processes generally ask for more information than necessary at this first step, hence lengthening the processing time unnecessarily. If fluctuations in customer demands were monitored, the manning levels can be adjusted to match the requirements. This requires a workforce that is not only multi-skilled but also flexible; which bring up the next problem.

3. Create Work Cells

Most government value streams are organized around separate departments and functions. For example, to obtain a government approval for a permit, an application form probably has to flow through no less than three separate departments and/or functions prior to approval. The main reason is because people performing a particular type of function are normally grouped together in the same place; because of this, in most government setups, there is a type of internal post office system (registry process) that handles this movement of work from one part of the organization to another. From a Lean perspective, this creates waste of transportation and waiting. In some government processes studied, this registry process makes at most three to four collections and deliveries a workday. Collected work-in-process is sorted according to destination and delivered at the next allocated time slot. This causes two problems; a waste of time managing the movement of work-in-process between processes and, more severely, the creation of a natural batch of work that kills the one-piece flow capability of the receiving processing step.

The solution to this kind of problem is deceptively simple. Why not create a work cell where all the necessary value-adding processing steps and personnel are located together? This cuts out the need for the registry process, which should take out 50 percent of the total processing time and allow for smoother work flow because batching is no longer required. Implementing this kind of solution has proven to be remarkable difficult, largely because of the mindset that says jobs of the same function should be clustered together.

A key feature of Lean work cells is the training of multi-skilled and flexible workers. In a Lean work cell, the goal is to have all workers trained to a level where everyone can perform the job at every workstation. Since everyone can do every job, processes are never left half finished because the right person to do a particular job is not around.

4. Eliminate Batching Work and Multi-Tasking

Because work within most governments is organized around functions and not around processes, most government officials are required to multi-task. Most government officials, at all levels, participate in more than one value stream. They also have a whole host of other types of work that takes them away from the main value-creating work streams (normally meetings and more meetings). To compensate for this, most government personnel batch their work; often waiting for a minimum number of work items to build-up before working on them.

This strategy increases their personal efficiency. Obviously it is more efficient to process a batch of similar type of work within a compressed time slot than to process them as they arrive. This is because batching eliminates the need for several set-ups. (It is a common perception that administrative work requires no set-up time. Anyone who has done administrative work knows that this is not true. Every time a particular type of work is to be performed, the processing officer needs at least the time to adjust their mind to that new type of work); however, the whole batching problem and the time it takes can easily be eliminated if work is organized around work cells. But, as noted, work cells are not easy to create in governments.

5. Enforce First in, First out

In manufacturing, "first in, first out" (FIFO) is the normal rule applied to the processing order of work.

If a company does not adhere to FIFO, much variation is added into the total distribution of processing time. For instance, in a last-in-first-out system, the jobs that come in last are processed quickly while the jobs that come in first take much longer to process.

Normally, in manufacturing value streams, there are FIFO lanes that prevent the FIFO rule from being violated. In government processes, jobs are often delivered into an in-tray. The in-tray creates a natural last-in-first-out effect leading to large overall processing time fluctuations. Large overall processing time fluctuations make the overall process less capable of meeting customer requirements as a whole.

The solution is once again the creation of Lean work cells, where work is pulled from one processing step to the next rather than pushed. If work is always pulled (that is, work is only ordered from the previous processing step when the operator is free), the FIFO rule will always be adhered to. Once again, the move from a push culture towards a pull culture is difficult for most governments. The normal government manager's mindset is to load people with more work than they can do so as to ensure that they are always occupied.

6. Implement Standardized Work and Load Levelling

Related to first-in-first-out issue is the lack of understanding and application of standardized work within government value streams. Even in highly repeatable work, it is fairly common to find different government workers performing similar tasks using slightly different methods and time. Because work is not standardized, there is no basis for evaluation and improvement. Often, the "best" workers are loaded with more work because they work faster and more efficiently than other workers. Overall and over time, this encourages government workers to slow their pace. They learn that additional work will be pushed to them once they complete a certain amount of their current workload. Hence, production is paced according to what is deemed reasonable by the supervisor and not paced according to customer demands.

7. Do Today's Work Today

Most government officials do not believe that work that arrives today can be finished today. They are correct to believe so because the way the work streams are currently set up do not allow work that arrives today to be complete on the same day. Over time, this cultivates a mindset that says, "We can always do it tomorrow."

What many governments may not realize is that customer demands remain largely constant from day to day. That is, the number of people applying for a particular permit each day tends to average out. If about 300 apply on Monday, a similar number are like to apply on Tuesday. If the government agency only managed to process 100 out of the 300 applications on Monday, there will be about 500 applications waiting to be processed on Tuesday (200 from previous day).

The accumulation of work-in-process has the effect of lengthening the expected flow time of the job. When the work-in-process is only 300, one can reasonably expect the permit to be processed within three days; however, by the end of the month, with work-in-process levels at 5,900, one can only expect their permit to be processed after 59 days and the problem continues to grow. The only way to stop this is to design value streams that can complete what comes in by the same day.

8. Make the Value Stream Visible

Last but certainly not least, the easiest way toward Lean governments is to teach government officials value stream mapping. Unlike manufacturing, there is no visible line in government. In fact, most people working in government do not even know they are part of a larger value stream. They think largely in terms of their job and their function. Making the value stream visible through value stream mapping exposes non-valued steps, time wasted by transportation and work-in-process, excessive process variation caused by non-standard work processes and production rules, waste caused by rework, waste caused by excessive checking and more. When a value stream map is created for their operations, many government officials are surprised by how much time and money is wasted. They also are surprised by how easy it is, once the value stream is visualized, to produce Lean government value streams.

Chapter 11: Applying Lean to the Public Sector

Governments at all levels must deliver more for less.

Governments around the world want to deliver better education, better health care, better pensions, and better transportation services. They know that impatient electorates expect to see change, and fast. But the funds required to meet such expectations are enormous; particularly in the many developed economies where populations are aging and the public sector's productivity hasn't kept pace with that of the private sector. The need to get value for money from governments at all levels is therefore under the spotlight as never before. But cost-cutting programs that seek savings of 1 to 3 percent a year will not be enough and in some cases may even weaken the quality of service.

To address the problem, public-sector leaders are looking with growing interest at "lean" techniques long used in private industry. From the repair of military vehicles to the processing of income tax returns, from surgery to urban planning, lean is showing that it can not only improve public services but also transform them for the better. Crucially for the public sector, a lean approach breaks with the prevailing view that there has to be a trade-off between the quality of public services and the cost of providing them.

By improving an "operating system" the configuration of assets, material resources, and staff a lean approach can cut costs dramatically, typically by 15 to 30 percent. But cost savings are only part of lean's appeal, as demonstrated by the experience of Toyota Motor, the pioneer of these techniques in the 1950s and the only consistently profitable volume car manufacturer. Lean aims to optimize costs, quality, and customer service constantly. It does so by engaging and equipping employees to focus on creating and delivering value in the eyes of the customer and eliminating whatever doesn't contribute to this goal. Contrary to popular belief, lean is about making a process or operation "fighting fit," not about cutting it to the bone.

Many businesses have followed Toyota's lead and undergone a lean transformation. A major European telecommunications company, for example, successfully applied lean techniques to a problem that was leading many of its customers to switch to competitors; the repair of faulty telephone lines. The company found that its call centre operators, diagnostics experts, and repair technicians operated as though they actually worked for rival employers. As a result, it took an average of 19 hours to repair a line. Using lean principles, the company realigned its organization and invested in the development of team leaders. In the first few months of its pilot project, productivity increased by 40 percent and recurring failures fell by 50 percent. The program was then rolled out across the company's national network, where it achieved similar success. Likewise, a major European bank used lean techniques to reduce the processing time for mortgage applications to 5 days, from 35; because fewer applicants dropped out of the process, the bank's revenues grew by 5 percent even as processing costs fell by 35 percent.

Is any of this relevant to the public sector? Not surprisingly, the concept and language of lean, rooted as they are in manufacturing, spark cynicism among many civil servants. Some feel that their priority should be matters of policy, not operations; others resent the notion that they are somehow part of a production line. Moreover, without the incentive of the profit motive, these government managers may believe they have neither a reason nor the levers to pursue a lean approach.

Yet practical experience suggests that they can. In a UK government office processing large volumes of standard documents, lean techniques achieved double-digit productivity gains in the number of documents processed per hour and improved customer service by slashing lead times to fewer than 12 days, from about 40, thus eliminating backlogs. The proportion of documents processed correctly the first time increased by roughly 30 percent; lead times to process incoming mail decreased to 2 days, from 15; and the staff occasionally attains the nirvana of an unprecedented zero backlog. In a UK military armoured-vehicle repair shop, a lean transformation generated a 44 percent increase in the availability of equipment, a 16 percent reduction in turnaround times, and a more than 40 percent increase in "right the first time" production. This achievement put about 40 more vehicles into operation at any one time. Moreover, the repair shop progressed from constantly missing its vehicle delivery deadlines to never missing them.

Persuading people to embark on the lean journey, where the last stop may be their own removal or reassignment, isn't easy. To succeed, public-sector organizations must find a way to align their growth strategy; providing new and better services at limited cost with a regard for the interests of their workers. Although lean programs may cut the number of public-sector jobs, the goal is to make the remaining ones more rewarding. Incentives come from the prospect of more meaningful work, potentially with room for greater autonomy or a chance to develop new skills.

To be sure, some countries bar layoffs (redundancies) of public-sector workers. In other cases, union contracts make layoffs difficult. Even so, increasing operational effectiveness can free employees from one part of an organization to deliver new or better services in other areas, within existing budgets and without layoffs. For instance, in Germany, Berlin's state government, which is barred by law from firing its workers, took an innovative approach; people no longer needed in one area were placed in labour pools where they could be selected for new assignments in others. Even in the United Kingdom, where workforce rules are more flexible, the government reinvests much of the money saved through efficiencies in new services, and workers often take on new roles.

Organizations can apply lean principles in almost any environment where a process can be defined at the working level. Many public services; military logistics, employment agencies, hospital tests, social-security benefits, airport security checks use processes that lend themselves to efficiency and quality improvements. Lean principles even apply in specialized fields such as legal casework and the development of policy. Work in these areas tends to be solitary, and the availability of e-mail and voice mail discourages face-to-face collaboration. Looking at such activities through a lean lens suggests that productivity can rise through more highly structured problem solving in teams, a more flexible allocation of resources, and a more sophisticated approach to managing knowledge. From an operational viewpoint, the aim is to smooth out the work flow.

The public-sector challenge

A lean system is designed to eliminate waste, variability, and inflexibility; though given the variety and complexity of many processes there can be no one-size-fits-all lean template. The needs of customers and the organization's goals and values drive the design. But some important themes and principles of the lean approach do pose specific challenges for public-sector organizations.

Taking the customer's perspective

All activities must be tested to ensure that they add value for the customer. Double-checking to be sure that they do reminds the organization of its purpose and ensures that processes are efficient. A car manufacturer or a retailer that fails to add value finds that its customers go elsewhere. But in government departments and other public organizations, putting customers first (even if you could identify them) may be more difficult.

One reason is a lack of competition. Customers of the government job seekers or patients, for example usually have no choice of provider. The demands of the customer, who may never even appear in the office, rarely come into focus. Much of the public sector remains supplier led, not customer led. But this norm could be changing. In the United Kingdom, for example, the government is introducing reforms that would allow people to choose where they go for medical treatment. Funding would follow the patient.

Still, most public organizations do not have the agility or frontline empowerment to respond to the changing demands of their customers. Systems committed to universal access, such as the United Kingdom's National Health Service (NHS), do not have the luxury of refusing to serve a particular segment.

Defining value for customers in the public sector can also be elusive. Costs, quality, and lead times are all important considerations in a lean system, but social value and the equitable provision of services are more difficult to measure. In health care, for example, how can a government balance the desire to give current patients the best possible treatment with the need to deliver care to people still on the waiting list?

One way to identify and then focus on the customer is to discuss these issues with the staff, ensuring that any improvement effort is framed with the customer very much in mind. Even in processes such as the criminal-justice system, counting the accused person as the customer is necessary to reframe and challenge traditional ideas and approaches.

Defining and managing end-to-end processes

The developers of a lean system identify end-to-end processes from a customer's perspective and then design and manage the system to keep information and materials flowing smoothly through those processes; however, public-sector managers sometimes lack the skills, experience, and mind-set to take this approach.

As in the private sector, the only way to understand and manage a process is to see how it works. Yet public-sector managers don't always see themselves as supervising or managing an "operation," and it is unusual for a single person to be responsible for an entire process. In addition, top-down targets tend to focus on a single part of the operation, to the detriment of the process as a whole. One mail-sorting facility, for example, set a target for dealing with incoming mail. The target diverted attention from outgoing mail, which sat in out trays for over two days.

A similar charge has been levelled at the requirement that 98 percent of accident and emergency patients in the United Kingdom must receive treatment within four hours. The risk is that local hospitals may merely shift the problem elsewhere; for example, by admitting patients to a holding ward to circumvent the four-hour deadline.

Compounding these difficulties is the growing propensity of governments to use outsourcing as a cost-cutting measure without always considering the impact of the outsourced service on the overall process flow. Outsourcing the work of hospital orderlies or transportation and logistics in a supply chain may reduce the fixed and variable costs of that particular activity. Yet these moves may drive up total costs and reduce the quality of service. Simply going for savings in one part of an organization may fail to improve its overall performance.

For all these reasons, senior executives must learn the details of any process for which they are accountable. In many cases, senior managers and executives are flying blind or, at best, relying on data and reports that fail to capture the complexity of the system and the experience of those working within it. To lead an organization that constantly strives to improve, the chief executive of a hospital, a social-service agency, or a prison must therefore spend at least one day a week on the "shop floor."

As work flows cut across organizational boundaries, it may be necessary to involve other departments or government agencies, possibly with different or even conflicting incentives. Consider the process of a trial. An effective process must deliver the defendant and all the relevant case information to court at the right time. As a minimum, the activities of the arresting officer, prison officials, prosecutors, victims, witnesses, and defence lawyers must be coordinated. Failures of coordination are common, leading to postponements, delayed judgments, and high opportunity costs.

To overcome such difficulties, decision makers should develop a shared understanding of the process. For the military repair shop mentioned earlier, this meant involving more than ten departments and other stakeholders in a steering group and ensuring that the goals of the transformation process reflected their varied desires. But competing interests sometimes impeded the overall process, underscoring the need for changes extending well beyond the gates of the repair depot.

Exposing and solving problems

A key characteristic of a lean organization is its ability to improve itself constantly by bringing problems to the surface and resolving them. Here as well the public sector often finds itself in a weaker starting position, with gaps in skills and entrenched mind-sets.

In a lean system, the surface-and-solve dynamic works in much the same way as lowered water levels expose sandbars in a river. For ships to navigate it without running aground, the sandbars must be dredged and the cycle repeated continually. The US Army Corps of Engineers has crews on the Mississippi, Ohio, and Illinois rivers from spring through November, dredging sandbars to keep the shipping channels open.

Many organizations keep their "water levels" high and deal with problems only if they break the surface. Such a system masks underlying problems. Rather than removing them, managers in the public sector are often tempted to add something to the system. Government departments around the world have, for example, tried to improve their processes by installing expensive IT systems. Many have delivered benefits; some, such as the case-management system of the US Federal Bureau of Investigation, have been expensive failures. Huge benefits probably would have been more likely even without the new IT systems if government managers had tackled the underlying process problems.

Moving from putting bandages over problems to solving them is particularly difficult in civil-service organizations because of a skill gap. Except in the military, operations management has not traditionally been a career path leading to the top tier of public service. Moreover, high-ranking civil servants tend to be organizationally and culturally removed from the delivery of frontline services, so policies are often made without a clear understanding of their effect on customers.

What is more, government reform programs are now under increasing scrutiny, which makes it difficult to uncover problems without embarrassment. A long-tenured manager needs courage to expose the waste that lies within his or her department or the deep-seated nature of its problems, especially if they can be resolved at little or no cost. The likely response will be, "If it was that cheap to fix, why wasn't it fixed before?"

Confronting such issues will demand brave leadership. Uncovering systemic problems within the public sector must become more politically acceptable; perhaps electorates will need to approve a "waste amnesty."

Developing a performance culture

When improving long-term performance is the goal, changing the process or the operating system will not suffice. The organization's culture must also change.

Some of these changes will be wrenching. A lean process, for example, requires a performance-tracking system that breaks down top-level objectives into clear, measurable targets that workers at every level must understand, accept, and meet. When performance isn't up to the standard, action is required. Tackling problems quickly and holding colleagues accountable for poor performance raises efficiency as well as moral. A lean process also tends to address the problem of "sticky" resources, prompting organizations to allocate them to shifting priorities more flexibly.

To mitigate the top-down nature of target setting, managers must often make changes themselves. In so doing, they should address the long-standing complaints of the frontline staff; complaints that typically include management's lack of engagement, a greater desire for teamwork, and the need to tackle underperformance.

Profound cultural changes generally follow and reinforce the lean transformation. The organization's moral rises as participants build capabilities and see others developing as well. Consider the processing of documents in the UK government office discussed earlier. Before the change, employees worked largely alone, processing batches at their own convenience. After the lean transformation, they began working as a team, which made everyone's activities transparent. Every team member helped to solve problems when performance dipped, and everyone worked together to identify opportunities for further improvement. The new mind-set, brought on by the lean reconfiguration, contributed to a 60 percent increase in productivity. This new transparency, however, also raised a whole new set of tough questions, including, "What should our performance targets be?" and "What happens when those targets are not met?"

Applying lean is difficult in the private sector, and more so in the public sector. Successful lean transformations must close the capability gap early in the process, so managers and staff can make the transition to a new way of working. Closing the gap typically involves hiring a few people with lean expertise and experience from outside the public sector to seed the transformation and build new internal capabilities.

Lean requires more than the courage to uncover deep-seated organizational problems; it may call for the ability to deal with job losses as well. Without ducking this simple truth, politicians and public-sector leaders must outline the need for change, explaining its benefits and the logic of the planned approach. They need to tell all stakeholders, including civil servants and the public, a compelling story about the impact and long-term benefits of change. The challenge to do more with less will not go away. A lean approach, with its emphasis on lower costs but higher quality and customer service, is surely worth investigating.

Chapter 12: Lessons of Lean

Lean could help public sector organisations deliver improved services whilst meeting government cost reduction targets.

The release of the Operational Efficiency Programme review, combined with spending pressures, has pushed Lean to the top of the public sector management agenda.

The need to deliver cost savings is not, however, a reason to jump on the Lean bandwagon. When used for what it was intended, the case for Lean is compelling; improved service at a lower cost delivered by an engaged workforce.

With the government's high spending, rising debt and a decline in GDP, public sector organisations are under pressure to reduce costs. The release of the Treasury's Operational Efficiency Programme review has further intensified this pressure.

There are, however, perceptions that to cut cost automatically means poorer service quality, a point of view echoed, in our experience, throughout many parts of the public sector. Yet, we who work within Lean enterprises would strongly disagree. In our world, good operational management is aimed at delivering efficiency. By that, we mean we aim to deliver the best service we can at the lowest possible cost.

Our proposition is that it is possible for all public sector departments to strive to achieve a balance of great service at acceptable costs. To achieve this, requires a change in mindset. In particular, it requires public sector managers to embrace integrated management systems such as Lean.

In the public sector, there are unanswered questions about the effectiveness of Lean in delivering greater efficiency, particularly, outside the large transactional process departments.

So, are all Government departments able to achieve levels of performance and customer satisfaction and is Lean the right system for them too?

In our view, the answer to both questions is "Yes", but we qualify this view by sharing five hard-learned lessons.

1. Lean is not a quick fix and is definitely not just a cost reduction tool.

2. Lean requires change to every part of an organisation.

3. Lean requires a very significant commitment from senior executives.

4. Lean starts with a deep understanding of, and commitment to, customers.

5. Lean won't work if you don't free your staff to help you improve your business.

If these lessons are applied correctly, then yes, Lean is capable of transforming organisational performance for the better, and can be successful in any public sector department.

1. Lean is not a quick fix and is definitely not just a cost reduction tool.

Having spent half a century perfecting their lean system, Toyota still consider themselves to be on the journey to operational excellence. On the other hand, we have had one client tell us "we tried Lean last year, but it didn't really work so we stopped".

Lean is a systemic, focussed and disruptive change. It requires time, patience and dedication to implement an integrated Lean solution.

There is no doubt that some Lean tools are good at improving process efficiency and reducing costs. Tools like seven wastes (a method by which one categorises non-value adding activities) spring to mind. Yet, using tools in isolation, without understanding of the operational context and business objectives, will often lead to fragmented solutions. This will dramatically reduce Lean's chance of achieving its full transformational potential.

2. Lean requires change to every part of an organisation.

Lean managers look critically at the whole organisational system. We call this "seeing the whole", but we do not take the business process reengineering, approach of, 'change everything all at once'. Change in Lean organisations is a constant process in which all managers and staff engage, driving out waste by generating huge numbers of sometimes small improvements to ways of working. At one point, Toyota claimed to be implementing two million ideas each year that had been generated by their staff.

The Lean approach must also acknowledge that localised improvement efforts can impact other parts of the system and no one department, team or business unit can get there on their own.

Lean should seek to test the extent that organisational targets are focused on increasing customer value and to baseline operational performance against the measures that matter, which may include:
    a. Customer service delivery and satisfaction.
    b. Quality and right first time.
    c. End to end process lead times and productivity.
    d. Extent to which organisational; capacity is aligned to customer demand.
    e. Staff satisfaction and engagement.
    f. Continuous improvement and change capabilities.

By doing this, a public sector organisation can start any Lean transformation from a threshold of performance; a level of performance where improvement directly corresponds to increased customer value.

3. Lean requires a very significant commitment from senior executives.

We have never seen a Lean system succeed without the total commitment of the senior team. We don't mean that CEO should send out a monthly newsletter; we mean that the entire top team (at least three layers deep) lives and breathes Lean.

They lead their teams in driving change by understanding customers better, by coaching and facilitating problem solving problems on the shop floor, by rewarding successes, by recognising great ideas and by behaving in a 'lean way'.

This means going beyond a simple technical or tools-based definition of Lean. It means addressing challenges such as transformational leadership; creating the capability within managers to create a vision and strategy for end to end change.

The departments that are seeing benefits across their entire organisation (back office, front office, and support functions) are those that have been able to secure senior management commitment and have set ambitious performance improvement targets.

One of our clients said; "In hindsight, we did not do enough to get senior management buy-in. Making senior managers aware of the changes that Lean will bring, alone, is not sufficient. We need to set ambitious goals and develop the capability in our managers to lead transformational change".

4. Lean starts with a deep understanding of, and commitment to, customers.

It has been our experience that public sector organisations have very limited understanding of the needs of their customers and, in fact, are often confused about who their customer is.

We once asked a senior operations manager in a Government department, "who is your key customer?" and were told 'the minister'!

Yes, the stakeholder map can be complex and in some organisations the normal rules do not apply but in general the public sector serves those members of the public who come to it and ask for services or products. We do not argue that this is always right, but it is a very good starting point.

Understanding the drivers of customer value can also be difficult. Feedback from customers is often limited to an annual satisfaction survey. This is not at a sufficiently granular level to drive operational service improvement. Our impression is that few public sector organisations have gained insight into customer views on the relative importance of the various value drivers or their observations of the organisation's current performance in relation to these key drivers.

We think that customer feedback should look to identify the detailed causes of "failure demand", that is demand that is placed on the operation as a result of poor initial service.

This generates additional work for the organisation. At one recent client, over 30% of calls placed into a call centre originated because customers could not understand the application forms. Here, we see an alignment of interests and creation of value; fix this problem and the customer gets a high quality service and the organisation reduces its costs.

Such types of customer insight can be delivered through voice of the customer analysis, including the investigation of customer complaints, failure and value demand analysis, and proactive tools such customer survey and focus groups.

We particularly like the very simple techniques of bringing customers together with operational staff, as part of performance improvement events, to ask.

"What is it like coming here for help?" Try it, you will be amazed at how staff are affected by the answers and how they then go back to work and set out to improve the customers' experience.

5. Lean won't work if you do not free your staff to help you improve your business.

Continuous improvement is the lifeblood of any Lean transformation; however, building a culture of continuous improvement is a significant challenge to any organisation that wants to be Lean.

We have seen recent examples across the public sector where, once the early enthusiasm for Lean or the 'big idea' wanes, performance drops as teams return to the older, more comfortable way of working.

Without overcoming these types of challenges, the benefits of any Lean change programme will be quickly undermined.

A more sustainable approach will require changes to organisational mindsets and ways of working. Part of the answer will be building and supporting continuous improvement processes which are based on identifying and improving operational problems in a structured manner.

This needs to start bottom up and may require the introduction of Lean through a series of cell-based pilots (a manageable team that is co-located around a product, customer outcome and process with supporting infrastructure).

By building continuous improvement with front-line teams, anticipated outcomes from this type of approach would include:
    a. Making visible and demonstrating at team level, the culture and organisational mindset required to sustain Lean.
    b. Implementing new approaches to structured problem solving.
    c. Establishing new accountabilities for performance management.

Each approach to Lean varies and needs to be adaptable. They are broad in scope and difficult to define precisely. We are passionate about Lean, because if applied effectively it helps managers and staff to deliver great service to customers without wasting resources on tasks that no-one values, whilst providing staff with the means to contribute to the improvement of their organisation; however, to be successful in any public sector department managers need to apply the five lessons we outlined in this chapter.

For those public sector organisations that can apply Lean in this way, the benefits are transformative change; improved customer service, at a lower cost, delivered in a sustainable way.

Chapter 13: Why Every Government Should Embrace Lean

The increasing pressure on every single department and agency across all levels of the public sector requires making major changes in the way government has operated in the past. Lean principles are often thought of as related to manufacturing. Every activity is part of a process, and lean teaches us that any process, and not just the manufacturing process, can be improved using lean thinking. Many in manufacturing have started on this journey to lean, but the government has yet to embrace it. Manufacturing organizations have shaved off 30 percent, 40 percent or even more from process costs by simply eliminating waste from the process. There is no excuse why people in the government sector cannot do the same. Lean thinking has grown from a paradigm shift in the manufacturing domain to a revolutionary approach in business processes in every industry.

The beauty of the lean process using Kaizen philosophy is the fact that it can benefit any kind of process or service. As a matter of fact, its application to government services is much easier than the manufacturing processes; just make sure that everyone is involved in route cause fact findings of the problem you are trying to improve before implementing kaizen. The lean process or the philosophy of Kaizen embodies all the notions of total quality control, continuous process improvement, zero-error production, and just-in-time production, and takes a holistic approach to foster improvements without large capital improvements. Lean process implementation consistently improves productivity and reduces costs through the optimization of facilities, people, resources and equipment.

Kaizen the philosophy that whatever you are doing, you can do better drives the lean thinking process. Kaizen is a Japanese word meaning never-ending improvement in home life, social life and working life. Whether one calls it world-class service, lean, or Kaizen, it is the most remarkable cost-reduction business operating or service delivery strategy of the 20th Century and it is beautifully simple. Toyota embraced the Kaizen philosophy-based lean system that has taken them from eradication to a world-class competitor and envy of the entire world as a class act to follow. While all lean system techniques are designed to eliminate waste, they are also intended to develop direct action for people to function autonomously, both running processes and improving them.

Lean process thinking provides a way to specify value, line up value-creating actions in the best sequence, conduct these activities without interruption whenever someone requests them, and perform them more and more effectively.

In short, lean thinking is lean because it provides a way to do more with less human effort, less equipment, less time, less space while coming closer and closer to providing customers with exactly what they want.

By closely observing the activities at the workplace, a supervisor and/or an employee can often identify areas that can be readily changed and improved with little or no cost to the service organization.

The lean process identifies and eliminates waste (activities that add no value or little value) by using a series of techniques to continuously improve the service as needed or requested by the customer. It provides speed and responsiveness, maximizing customer satisfaction by improving quality, reducing cost, and meeting customer delivery requirements.

Lean processes focus on elimination of all waste, in every process. The result is our ability to produce services in the most efficient way and ensure quality and on-time delivery for every customer.

When a maintenance mechanic walks a long distance with a tool in his hand, he is adding no value to the service. When the driver waits a half-hour while the vehicle is being repaired, the waiting adds no value to the service. Work is a series of processes or steps, starting with raw material and ending in a final product or service. At each step value is added to the product, to the service being performed, or to the document being processed and then sent to the next step of the process. The resources utilized at each process people or machines either add value or no value. Any activity that adds no value is waste.

What does "value-added" mean? Any activity that changes material, moves or transforms material, or changes or provides information by producing something that the customer requires, is value-added activity. An activity is value-added if.
1. The customer recognizes the value and is willing to pay for it, e.g., taxpayer is willing to pay for garbage collection.
2. The product/service or information physically changes or work is produced during the process, e.g., filling the pothole with asphalt, creating a schematic, or filling information on a form.
3. The activity must be done right the first time, e.g., all rework is non-value-added or waste. Lean process thinking relentlessly pursues systematic waste reduction. If the customer wants a five-page report and the worker prepares a seven-page report, that is waste.

As mentioned above, everything that does not directly transform material or information to create value for the customer or the taxpayer is waste. This does not mean the activity isn't necessary however, waste shows up throughout processes and minimization of that waste is how you move towards ideal conditions. If you cannot eliminate the waste, then don't quit; start reducing. If you do this relentlessly, continuously and daily, you will have a much higher ratio of value-added to non-value-added work. The greatest leverage in the war against waste exists in the upfront design and planning process.

Chapter 14: Improving Value Creating Processes

Over 10 years ago a friend of mine got a call from the mayor of a major American city who told him he wanted to create the first "lean" city government. What this might mean was unclear to my friend. He knew nothing about his city and had done no thinking about lean in government at any level. So he went to see him and they had some fun looking at a couple of sample processes; arresting vagrants and processing building permits.

They put a brief effort into taking gemba walks along both value streams, discovering that the best thing to do with vagrants was to create a separate process (a vagrant product family if you will) that was quick, simple, and removed from the arrest process for actual criminals. (This meant the vagrants could be treated more humanely and officers could get back on the streets much more quickly. The important question of whether vagrants should be arrested at all was left for another time.)

By contrast, issuing building permits in this growth-oriented city was straightforward. Rather than asking contractors to come to city hall in the middle of a vast metropolitan area far removed from where buildings were actually being built, it made more sense to create four processing centres in the four quadrants of the city and instead of sending the permit requests through four different departments, with queues and delays in each department, the countermeasure was to collocate the parts of each department concerned with permits, and pass the applications around a table, pretty much in single-piece flow. It seemed possible to reduce the wait time for a building permit from a month to a day.

So far, so good. But then bureaucracy and politics came into play. The mayor had a limited attention span. I am being generous and no one was given responsibility for overseeing the new processes and perfecting the flow of value across different departments. Then, it turned out that resources were needed to do rigorous experiments to test the ideas, and the project had to be put out to public bids a process that was a nightmare. Ultimately, nothing much could be done or sustained by the earnest line managers without continuing upper-level support and everyone gave up.

A few years ago another friend of mine was asked to spend a day in Australia at the City of Melbourne (which is as Manhattan is to New York City, the office tower centre of a vast metropolitan area). This time my friend was also asked to walk two processes; writing parking tickets (and collecting the money) and planning events (like concerts) in city parks. It was a totally different world.

In each case a team of representatives from all of the departments and divisions involved had mapped the current process, identified the gap in performance, envisioned a better process, and started a series of PDCA (Plan, Do, Check, Act) cycles to close the gap.

Everything was visual, showing clear responsibility for the performance of each value stream and its improvement across departments. My friend had the strong sense that the progress the teams were making could be sustained, with standardized work for managers and front-line workers.

The one problem that had arisen was that when a city becomes really, really good at ticketing every vehicle that overstays its parking time by more than five minutes, motorists become really, really good at not overstaying their time. As a result ticket revenues were falling even as other objectives for an improved value stream; better availability of parking spaces and a much better system for resolving disputes about broken meters and traffic officer behaviour were being achieved. This was another example of how every countermeasure designed to improve a value stream creates unintended consequences, which must in turn be counter measured. It is a normal part of any improvement process.

The Melbourne experience, along with a number of recent calls I have gotten from state and local governments asking about lean thinking and the fact that governments everywhere are facing growing financial pressures at the same time voters expect better performance, have led me to think again about ways that lean principles and methods might be applied to the activities of governments.

Let's start with what governments do. What value do they try to create? I think there are really three streams of work; enacting policies (laws) to regulate behaviours or deliver services; designing the enforcement and delivery mechanisms for these policies; and, operating these mechanisms on a continuing basis.

A simple example. A government (legislative plus executive) enacts environmental rules to address a perceived problem, a state agency writes detailed regulations and designs a mechanism for enforcement (e.g., granting permits), and the agency processes permits and proceeds against individuals and organizations who fail to comply with the rules. This is a vast activity, a substantial part of Gross National Product in every country, and one that seems to grow everywhere. (The Code of Federal Regulations in the United States, which records the detailed provisions of each federal law, now has more than 170,000 pages of text. State and local statutes and regulations contribute many times more.)

The first of these activities enacting laws is clearly the most problematic. What a wonderful thing it would be if every public discussion of an issue was in the form of an A3! (If Newt Gingrich could run for president in 2012 on the platform of "Lean Six Sigma for Every Government Activity," perhaps someone in the Lean Community should be running for USA president in 2016 on the platform of "A3 for All?". The objective would be to describe what every public issue is about in one sentence, assess whether the problem needs to be addressed (or an opportunity needs to be seized), determine the root cause of the issue, detail the most promising countermeasures to test through PDCA, and identify what evidence will be accepted as to the success of the countermeasures.

Most Americans are familiar with the phrase that "the states are the laboratory of democracy" because of their freedom to try different countermeasures for the same problem. This is even more true of local governments. So there are three levels of government available for doing science. The problem is the will to do so.

The way things actually work is that all political debates start with solutions and work backwards to problems. We can be sure that every solution is being promoted by someone with an emotional stake in the outcome ("save the planet" by regulating greenhouse gases) or with money to gain (for example, by advocating for mandating a new "green" activity in which they have a large financial stake). Sometimes these can be combined, for example mandating the addition of a minimum amount of ethanol in gasoline before it can be sold to the public, which may save the planet and certainly makes money for corn growers.

To be clear. We in the Lean Community have no standing on whether a government should regulate any activity or provide any service. This is a decision for citizens and their lawmakers. We can only make the humble suggestion that better decisions can be reached if the debate starts with a clear statement of the actual problem, followed by a structured process to identify and test countermeasures. For example, we have no voice in whether governments should license drivers. (Some libertarians probably think they shouldn't; most people think they should.) But if governments are going to license drivers, we can suggest the important questions to ask. What is the best way to design and operate the drivers licensing process? How can we avoid wasting the time of the drivers and government employees while insuring that those who don't have the skills or wisdom to be on the road are not licensed?

Yet when I look at governments at every level today I observe that most issues are not clearly stated, regulatory and service provision processes are not designed using lean principles, and regulations and services are not administered or provided using lean methods. So what can be done?

A3 for the policy-making process may take a while (although I am always an optimist about the long run, as we demonstrate the power of this method in non-governmental activities). So I wouldn't wait around expecting progress in that area soon; but the prospect for improving the design of regulations and services is much brighter, as is the prospect for improving the actual conduct of regulation and the delivery of services. But, please, no "lean government" programs to be rolled by elected officials early in their terms, supported by a phalanx of consultants or internal staff teams committed to winning the "war on waste" in short order.

Instead the way ahead is to begin; any place will do with experiments involving line managers and employee teams (and, yes, the people being regulated or served by the value streams as well). In each experiment make someone responsible for leading the development of an A3 that determines the current performance of a given value stream (for arresting vagrants or issuing building permits or whatever). Post the results; the work, after all, is the public's business and is the business of the employees as well. Determine the gap in performance on whatever dimension is relevant; cost to the taxpayer, cost in wasted time to the person receiving the service, headaches for the government employees (or contractors) performing the work. Identify the most promising countermeasures. Run experiments with the countermeasures. Measure the results. Reflect on what to do next and, in particular, how to sustain positive results.

If any government at any level is willing to try this simple method for improving its value-creating processes, I will be delighted to take a gemba walk and help publicize the results. I am sure they will be highly positive.

Chapter 15: Pushing the Boundaries of Lean Management

Case Study: How does lean contribute to making Melbourne one of the world's most liveable cities year after year?

Words: Lean Program Manager, City of Melbourne

With its cosmopolitan lifestyle, abundant parks and gardens, well-designed streets and buildings, and a calendar full of major sporting, artistic and culinary events, Melbourne consistently rates at the top or near the top of international liveability indexes.

Employees at the City of Melbourne pride themselves as innovators who routinely re-imagine how cities can function better. So it was always going to be interesting when a new outsider CEO arrived, bringing with her lean thinking and a vision of how to reinvent not the city this time, but the organization itself.

The City of Melbourne is leading the way in applying lean to local government in Australia, having embarked on its lean journey in earnest in 2009. As it often happens in organizations in sectors relatively new to the methodology, City of Melbourne staff was sceptical of the method's application to local government and in the early years the sentence "It won't work in my area; we are different" was frequently heard; however, we persevered and now all 30 branches (departments) have applied lean within their service streams to make things better, faster, cheaper and easier for customers, staff, the organization and the community.

We have learned a great deal about how lean can benefit an organization that comprises many different businesses, where silo thinking prevails and politically-driven imperatives largely determine the focus of the organization.

Applying lean in a local government setting presents some challenges. I learned about lean during my time in healthcare and spent many years translating it from manufacturing widgets to caring for patients.

In healthcare the concept of customer is clear: it always comes back to the patient, and when you are making decisions, putting the patient at the centre of the decision making is somehow easier.

At the City of Melbourne we can get easily confused about our customers; is it the residents, the businesses in the city, or the thousands of people that come to the city every day to work and visit? What is good for one group is often not good for another.

Additionally, organizational direction can change quickly in a political environment, where elected councillors are responsible for the delivery of a four-year Council Plan.

But in many respects local government is not different from other sectors. There are high-volume services and processes that will continue no matter what the political agenda, and they should all be continually improved to deliver as much customer value as possible.

What is the Purpose of the Lean Transformation at city of Melbourne?

The lean transformation (CoMLean) is led by the CEO, Dr Kathy Alexander. At the beginning of her tenure in 2008, she promised her staff that there would be no external efficiency reviews on her watch.

A year earlier, following such a review, almost 100 employees (over 5% of the total workforce) were made redundant and the organization was restructured.

This resulted in short term savings at a cost that was almost half the savings, extremely low moral; delays in delivery of initiatives as everyone tried to work out who their new boss was and what their new jobs were. What the restructuring and cost reduction did not do was increasing the efficiency or the effectiveness of the organization. In fact, there were many areas where processes were made less efficient because of the loss of a staff member whose job had been to own a process and coordinate it across the organization.

Kathy was committed to improving the performance of the City of Melbourne both in terms of efficiency and quality. She had some knowledge of lean thinking from healthcare and within a few months she convinced her senior staff to try a couple of pilot projects.

One of the projects returned AU$800,000 in the first year and another improved a long-term senior executive problem; as a consequence, the organization agreed to experiment some more. By 2010, City of Melbourne was deeply committed to lean as an improvement methodology and established an internal team led by myself.

Four years on, the key purpose of the transformation at City of Melbourne is clear; supporting the organization in delivering more value-adding services in response to increased population and community demand within the existing staff base, wherever possible doing more with existing resources.

Comparing the number of rateable (taxable) properties within the city to the number of staff in the organization is a useful way for the City of Melbourne to measure its performance over time. This indicator is heading in the right direction to demonstrate productivity gains.

Starting with Process Improvement

A frequently asked question for new lean thinkers is "Where should we start?" It doesn't really matter where you start, just start somewhere.

We began our lean journey improving high-volume or problematic services and processes. The CEO and executives chose the first projects and then took responsibility for sponsoring these large-scale improvements, known as Director Streams. We quickly learned the benefits of getting everyone together to map the process, including those who do and lead the work, across the silos and including externally contracted service providers. This was the first step in connecting senior leaders to the problems that existed within organizational processes.

Over five years, we have worked on more than 20 large-scale improvement streams.

We avoid using the word project to describe continuous improvement because carrying out projects is high-volume work within the organization as a method of delivering the Council Plan. At the City of Melbourne, projects have a defined start and end, with an on-time and on-budget focus.

Staff initially thought about the lean work in the same way. They were keen to get the improvement projects finished, with little understanding of the fact that continuous improvement means ongoing improvement, underpinned by the PDCA cycle, for the life of the process.

For many of the processes and services improved so far, mapping revealed there was no standard way of performing the process or, if there was, often staff did not follow it. Few processes had good measures of performance so it was difficult to determine how well a process performed. Thus, much of the improvement work focused on developing a standard or agreed way of working and supporting its implementation.

We sought the voice of the customer to clarify value from a customer perspective and then used this information to develop value-based process measures. We found many processes lacked design, evolving over time, layer upon layer, often relying on the expertise of single individuals, with risk of corporate loss if that person left the organization.

Staff started to consistently look for waste in organizational processes, with defects and over processing "just in case" being the most common wastes identified. This look in the mirror was important for us as we gained a sense of the amount of effort that would be required to create stable processes that delivered on our purpose.

We thought; if the City of Melbourne is already regarded as a great organization, how much better could it be if our processes were more effective and efficient?

With thousands of processes in the organization, the road ahead seemed daunting and, with a small improvement team of four, the CEO and senior leaders realized that building capability across the organization was going to be paramount.

Engaging and Developing the people

Lean cannot be sustained by a centralized improvement team. It requires engagement and commitment from those who do the work as well as support of leaders, who are responsible for those who create real value for the customers of the organization. In 2011, engaging and developing staff in improvement commenced formally at the City of Melbourne. The Lean Learning Pathway has itself been the subject of improvement and PDCA based on participant feedback and observed outcomes of the learning in practice. All programs are developed and delivered in-house, using simulations based on local government processes.

For City of Melbourne staff, learning about lean starts at induction and continues through various levels until the Lean Practitioner status is reached. More than 50% (700) of staff has now completed Lean Basics, a one-day introductory course on lean principles, waste and A3 thinking.

More than 100 of these staff members have gone on to complete a Lean Learner qualification where they apply what they have learned to their work. The Lean Learners program provides support and guidance for individual staff to tackle their first A3 and has helped the organization demystify the art of A3 thinking and filling in those six boxes, a skill previously owned by the internal lean team.

I was somewhat sceptical about asking staff to work on an A3 after just one day of lean training (it took me years to appreciate A3 thinking) however, my team have proved me wrong. It can be done.

In fact I think this is the most significant step we have taken in the past year; developing deepening A3 thinking skills in operational staff, while cultivating a culture where staff are lining up to continue the lean learning pathway and we can't meet the demand. What a great problem to have!

Here are few examples of Lean Learner contributions to the City of Melbourne Lean win log.

1. Steve from Engineering Services, reduced the time it takes to replace residents existing garbage bins with larger bins by 30% (from 17 days to 12 days).

2. Melbourne visitor shuttle ticket stubs use to take 11 minutes per day to sort and reconcile. Kerry has reduced the time to 3 minutes a day, releasing 53 hours a year for value added work.

3. Emma from Parking and Traffic removed wasteful steps from the process of handbill rejection letters reducing the time taken from nine minutes to two minutes and releasing 140 hours of staff time per year.

Lean Practitioner is the next level of learning and is designed to equip leaders and senior operational staff to lead the lean effort within the organization. This course, developed in-house, has attracted more than 100 staff, with the status of Lean Practitioner highly regarded within the organization.

The 22-week course is hard work, with classroom teaching, weekly homework and reflections, a lean improvement project and an exam at the end of the course. Many lean champions are identified through this course and their contribution to the organization's journey of transformation has allowed us to test the concepts in almost all work environments.

In addition to building capability, Lean Practitioner has helped to break down barriers across a large, diverse and hierarchical organization, creating a common language across professional groups. In 2014, we gained certification of the Lean Practitioner course, which is now recognised by a local university. This means participants are rewarded with a formal qualification for their efforts in addition to the improvement they deliver to the organization.

Building Leadership and the Management System.

Lean at the City of Melbourne is led from the top. Kathy will admit she was new to the approach, however the more she experienced it, the more she became aware that lean needed to form the basis of the organization's leadership development system. To this end, in 2012 Kathy brought together the Lean Transformation, Organizational Development and Planning and Performance teams. Since that time, leadership programs have focused predominantly on developing lean thinking skills. Nine core leadership capabilities are now identified, with "leads improvement" and "develops and coaches others" articulated as the top two.

Kathy practices her lean leadership skills every day, replacing her notebook with a pad of A3s and her favourite coaching questions. She recently told me; "I learnt that I wasn't really coaching until I started asking the right questions".

The City of Melbourne has realized there is a lot to be done in relation to leadership development.

"Most efforts were previously focused on emerging leaders," said Tanya Athans, who leads the Organizational Development team. "We did not have a standard way of assessing and developing leaders that aligned with a lean organization. We still have a long way to go, but at least now we know where we want to get to and the path to get there is becoming clearer."

In 2013, senior leaders who had not engaged with lean took part in a new program called The Way We Work, which is a five-step process designed for any work area to help understand how to use lean as a management system. It begins and ends with the customer.

City of Melbourne Way of Working.

The 24 leaders who came together for the program worked to articulate clearly what the organization did; its core value streams. This thinking has proved extremely useful for an organization that a few years ago saw itself as 30 discrete and autonomous businesses, many of which had little in common. These value streams will be used going forward as the basis for thinking about processes and improvement efforts.

Guiding principles

What is the Basic Thinking that Drives Our Transformation.

The basic thinking that underpins the City of Melbourne lean transformation is A3 thinking. For an organization of innovators, coming to terms with deeply understanding the problem before thinking about a solution was difficult; however, the organization has made real progress with respect to this. "What problem are you trying to solve?" is a frequently heard comment around the executive table. The increased requirement for data and fact by the executive table drives lean analysis as part of the work the organization does every day, including requests for staff and new projects.

Going Forward

The impact of lean on how we now think and act as an organization was evident in our recent financial performance. At the Australasian Lean Thinking and Practice Summit, recently held in Melbourne, Kathy shared some of our progress with delegates. "Over the past two years, we have kept cost increases below inflation. During the same period we have built and staffed three new libraries, a new recreation centre;

we have run three new major events a year, doubled the sustainability program, introduced an urban forest program, expanded capital works and water saving programs while also accommodating the increased demand for human services resulting from a 20% population increase. During this time we have not reduced or ceased any service. Despite all of these new programs, the number of assessable properties per Full Time Equivalents has increased by 8% since 2010. Lean thinking supports our effort to do more with our existing resource base."

With thousands of processes across the organisation that represent endless opportunities for improvement, we constantly struggle with the question. "Are we working on the right thing?" Improving one process inevitably reveals another three we could improve, and maintaining performance in areas previously improved continues to challenge us; however, our focus on deep learning of the method is paying off and I liken it to making a patchwork quilt. We now have more people who can practise the craft so we are making more and more patches, whilst improving the quality of the patches. Our focus on purpose, people and process allows us to bring the patches together into something that will be functional (an effective and efficient organization) but also a work of art; a thriving, energetic organization of problem solvers who are constantly focused on making things better for customers.

Chapter 16: Lean Consumption at the Post Office

I was in the US last Year December; I went to the local post office to buy holiday stamps and Priority Mail boxes. (Priority Mail for gift parcels is a great deal; you can cram as much stuff as possible into your free "flat rate" box that will arrive in about 3 days; all for about the price of the box alone at the UPS Store.)

After waiting in line for 20 minutes, the clerk motioned me forward. (Note to self; avoid the Post Office at lunch time; half the clerks go on break just in time for their noon customer rush.)

"I did like to buy some Christmas stamps, please."

"I am sorry sir, we are out of holiday stamps."

"When will you get some more?" I asked hopefully.

"They are backordered now, but we should have them by the end of the month."

"But the end of the month is after Christmas." I said lamely.

"We have these salsa dance stamps; they have some nice holiday colours in them." the clerk suggested.

I appreciated the unexpected empathy; maybe the Post Office really does care. I pictured salsa dance stamps on my Christmas card envelopes and wondered if anyone would notice. Dancing is part of the holidays, isn't it? My mind went tilt. Next subject.

"Well, how about some flat rate Priority Mail boxes?" I needed to ship some Christmas gifts.

"I'm sorry, we are out. You can just use your own boxes and put Priority Mail stickers on them."

She didn't understand. Call me thrifty, but I like using the free Priority Mail boxes. Especially the flat rate variety that you can cram full with the heavy stuff for no extra charge. Besides, did I mention the price of boxes at the UPS Store?

I left empty handed. I was an eager customer thwarted from spending money.

The US Postal Service is experiencing monumental market shifts; email, on-line bill payment, FedEx Ground, UPS Stores, Google adwords. Their market share is shrinking all around. All that is left for them is neighbourhood junk circulars and holiday mail.

A good first step might be for the post office to stock stamps and boxes so I can do business with them. Maybe if the Postmaster General read this book, it would make a difference. I will get their lean transformation started and just mail him a copy myself…damn, I don't have any Priority Mail boxes!

Chapter 17: Canada Post Lean Transformation

Behind a dust barrier of orange plastic sheeting, workers with power tools disassemble the metal superstructure and chutes of a huge mechanical parcel sorting machine in the middle of Canada Post's Calgary plant. But the real demolition work here is being done by lean thinking.

The sorter, which required 58,000 square feet, eight operators, and a maze of conveyors to separate and route incoming parcels to their destinations, has been replaced by a nearby cell occupying just 12,000 square feet, staffed by six people sorting parcels manually, based on lean principles of takt time, flow, and balanced work. When the sorter is gone, the cell will move to a far edge of the sorter's former space, bringing parcel sorting operations much closer to a dock where trucks deliver and load parcels and mail.

The move will cut lead time and eliminate the need for much of the conveyor system, which will mean lower maintenance costs and fewer back injuries to employees who had to clear jammed parcels from conveyors and chutes.

A Closer Look

Like many services, postal operations look a lot different from traditional manufacturing. Manufacturing customers order finished goods from a plant, which orders raw materials from suppliers. In a postal service, paying customers are suppliers, pushing raw materials - mail - to plants, often with end customers not knowing that mail is coming or even wanting it. So at first glance, there appeared to be few if any opportunities to use lean techniques such as finished goods supermarkets, or levelled production. Since the "inventory" of mail already is paid for, moving it faster doesn't improve cash flow as in a traditional lean implementation.

But beginning in the mid-1990s officials at Canada Post began taking a closer look at their operations as part of a drive to cut costs and improve service. At the time, mail was moved in big batches from one production island, such as a sorter or other large machine, to the next machine, where it often waited and then was processed as fast as possible.

They discovered that such batch-and-queue postal operations had many of the wastes that lean production principles were designed to identify and eliminate from manufacturing. For example, letters and parcels, like parts, waited to be transported and processed. Large batches of mail, just like large batches of goods, required excess space, equipment and handling. (Moving mail faster doesn't improve cash flow, but it does reduce the number of containers, forklifts, and conveyers needed.) Postal activities, like their manufacturing counterparts, contained wasted motion.

Long changeovers on highly automated equipment increased lead-times. Miss-sorted letters or parcels were equivalent to defects and rework. While tools like supermarkets might not make sense in the postal environment, flow did. In fact, they discovered that flow and most lean principles applied to the post office's main mission of moving the mail.

"I used to think that we were not a manufacturing company; we didn't produce anything," said Director, mail operations, at the Calgary facility, "but you can lean out mail operations. What we were looking for is flow; in one door and out another." "What is interesting about our business is that pull system supermarkets don't apply so much," said Manager projects, at Calgary. "We look more at flow because we have no control over what comes in at any point in time. "Flow between processes is maintained by FIFO (first-in, first-out) lanes.

Calgary improvement teams pursued continuous flow in much the same way that any plant or office for that matter would. First, they identified product family value streams. They found four:
1. Letters
2. Parcels
3. Express mail
4. Publications and advertising mail ("Pubs and ad mail," as it is called, includes items such as magazines, catalogues, and marketing pieces.)

"Each value stream has had success with applying lean," said Director, mail operations. Here is a look at how it was done in pubs and ad mail.

Sweating the Details

About two years ago, an improvement team of managers and engineers believed a manual sorting cell could be designed to perform better and faster than the existing system in which mail bags in large metal containers or "cages" were removed from trucks, staged on the dock, and ultimately emptied through holes in the floor onto hidden conveyors. "The conveyors held all the product so you never saw your inventory," said Director, mail operations.

The conveyors took the bags to the sorting machine; operators at the sorter read the coded destination tags on bags and keyed them into the computer system, which routed the bags by conveyor to a big cart. Carts were taken to another area of the plant for further sorting to the final destination. "We handled the bags four times," he said. Besides being wasteful, multiple handling meant operators were repeatedly lifting the 50-to-60 pound bags.

The team used value-stream mapping and other tools to study the mail moving through the sorter and discovered it could be broken into four major groups based on its general destinations; eastern Canada, southern Alberta, the city of Calgary, and mixed mail that had to be sorted further. "Each of the four flows worked out to being almost exactly 25% of the volume," he said.

Next the team members calculated a takt time, the heartbeat of any lean system because it matches the rate of production to demand. They divided the amount of time in seconds on one shift, minus non-working time, by customer demand, defined as the normal volume of mail bags per day coming through the process.

"We came up with one bag every 24 seconds," he said. "If the volumes went up, all we had to do was run the cell longer. We had two more shifts to play with."

The next step was to identify and time the actual work elements performed by operators. This helped the team separate elements that added value from those that didn't; such as walking and eliminate the non-value-adding activities. Team members observed and timed operators lifting bags, reading destination tags, opening bags, dumping out the bundles of mail, reading addresses, tossing bundles of mail into containers, etc. Once the work elements and times were known, the team created an operator balance chart to staff the cell and distribute the work based on takt time.

In the new cell, metal cages containing mail bags are lined up in FIFO order in staging lanes across from the first operation, called "induction." Lanes are sized to hold approximately two hours of work. "Now the inventory is right in front of your eyes, not on hidden conveyors," he said. "When the work is visual, you know exactly what you have. You can plan your day.

The supervisors know how to staff better because at the beginning of a shift, they know how much work is there and how many people are needed for an area."

Every 24 seconds, the operator at the induction station removes a bag from a cage placed in a painted square adjacent to the belts. Using a new overhead robotic arm that eliminates bending and heavy lifting, the operator removes the bag, reads the destination tag and places it on one of four short conveyor belts, corresponding to each of the four major mail flows.

The conveyors move bags to nearby stations where operators open them and immediately sort the mail. Operators can move from one station to another to help clear a spike in mail volume.

Before the cell went live, the team constructed a mock-up off the plant floor where operators could try out the new process, get a feel for the pace of work, and offer suggestions. The team also developed standard work documents for each station that describe the major steps, including key points and safety tips. he said; the involvement and new robotic arm helped employees adjust to the cell. "I thought we did get some pushback but we didn't."

Sharing the expectation for the pace of work in the new cell turned out to be a valuable exercise, he said. In the unionized postal environment, managers worried about setting expectations for how much mail the cell should sort in a given amount of time. But the pace and visibility of the cell proved to be a benefit because employees as well as supervisors liked knowing what was expected and whether they were ahead or behind. In fact, operators had to learn that in the new system faster wasn't always better.

"At first, they thought they had to go as fast as possible to get mail into the cell, "he said. "We explained that if you put a bag into the cell every 24 seconds, the mail goes through faster and it saves us money. If you put a bag on every five seconds it plugs up the system."

Automation Advantages

Lean thinking also helped to unplug the jams in Calgary's highly automated systems in the value stream for letters. The first step in the process use machines that automatically cancel the stamps and orient the letters face up so the next machines in the process can read addresses, apply bar codes, and sort letters for shipment to destinations. Letters for Calgary remain in the plant for a final machine sort to carrier routes.

Traditionally, the hoppers feeding letters to machines at the first step were kept filled. An improvement team discovered that introducing smaller batches of mail more often led to fewer jams. So now a bag is dumped into the hopper every 35 seconds. The team also found that the machine could run faster and smoother if operators culled out large envelopes and sorted them separately. "A group of people got together and came up with these ideas," he said. "We said, Okay let's trust it because lean is working for us." The result is that letters arriving in the afternoon are sorted by 11p.m. that night instead of 3a.m. the next day.

Getting away from big batches is paying off at the final step where Calgary letters are sorted by route. The sorting machine reads bar codes applied in the previous step and deposits letters in small bins, each corresponding to a carrier's route. Calgary has roughly 1,800 routes, but the machines has only 180 bins, so "plans" or programs are needed to sort the city's letters. After each program ran, operator performed the equivalent of a changeover. They would "sweep' or clear the bins and load the next program. Loading a program was a computerized process that took just two minutes. But sweeping took 45 minutes, during which time the machine was idle.

"We used to run 30,000 or 40,000 pieces of mail in a plan, thinking that it was best to process a big batch to minimize the number of changeovers," he explained. "But you couldn't run more mail until the bins were empty or you did mix up routes."

By switching to smaller batches of letters and adjusting the programs to use half of the bins, an improvement team boosted performance. Now, while the sorter runs a program that is been adjusted to use 90 bins at one end of the machine, an operator sweeps letters from the 90 bins at the other end.

Programs were redesigned to put two routes instead of one in each of the 90 bins. An operator keeps them separate by inserting coloured plastic cards between the stack of letters for each route. The result is that the machine can run constantly, matching the throughput speed of 30,000 letters per hour of the previous sorting machine and reducing the inventory between steps.

"If you run 10,000 or 15,000 pieces of mail at a time it never fills up," he said. "And we now have no lost time due to changeovers."

Value-Stream Managers

Moving from a mindset of batching to flow required training. Few years ago, Calgary trained all its supervisors in the basics of lean and value-stream mapping. "Black belts," including the sites project manager, received extensive training in lean and six sigma. Explaining the difference in applying each, he said "if a sorting machine develops a high reject rate that inhibits flow, he applies six sigma tools to identify and eliminate the cause. Value-stream managers also have basic knowledge of mapping and lean so they can work with the black belts to redesign and improve value streams".

"Value stream managers focus on the end-to-end process, from the pick-up to the delivery of their value-stream products," he explained. "It improved our service dramatically."

When he arrived at Calgary in 1999 as day shift manager, and the two other shift managers were responsible for all the products on their shifts. A year-and-a-half later, the plant switched to value-stream managers responsible for their product families across all three shifts. As operations director, he added a new wrinkle by sending the managers outside the Calgary plant on visits to local postmasters.

"They had to go out and visit the small towns where their products went," he said. "They had to talk to the postmasters where we were failing miserably, watch their products arriving, and find out why we were failing. So, they really got end-to-end responsibility from induction at Calgary to where the mail is delivered."

Such exercises led directly to improvements at Calgary. Local postmasters knew mail was arriving miss-sorted, but couldn't tell why. When the value-stream managers saw the problem, they knew where it came from because they were familiar with the processes at the plant.

"We had to jump our continuous improvement effort up a notch," he said "We never would have done it if we hadn't sent the value-stream managers out to take a look."

Calgary is trying to extend the other end of the value stream, working with its big customers, the major mailers in Calgary. The city has the largest number of corporate headquarters in Canada after Toronto. Big customers are supposed to notify the plant when they are preparing a large mailing, such as bills to customers. Postal workers will pick up the mail in stages beginning earlier in the day to smooth the volume moving through the plant instead of having it arrive all at once.

Because Calgary is a growing city, thanks to the oil boom and a favourable tax structure, "our mail volumes are constantly growing," he explained. "We had to deal with that pressure and we didn't have a system to flow the mail through until we began implementing lean. Now we have something that works for us." he estimates Calgary is adding 18,000 addresses annually.

That kind of growth puts pressure on Calgary's 12 satellite postal facilities, called "depots" where mail carriers are based. "We were adding so many routes that these buildings were at maximum capacity and we were going to have to build more."

The Calgary plant has freed so much space; a total of 61,000 square feet so far, that Canada Post will move mail carrier operations into the freed space, and shrink from 12 small satellite offices to four larger ones. "So our operating maintenance costs will diminish, transportation costs will be cut, too, along with lease costs," he said. The challenge is to keep up with the growth while continuously improving by cutting costs, he said.

Director of logistics and processing improvement, at Canada Post said the effort is paying off companywide since Tom Charlton, the company's retired senior vice-president of operations, became interested in the postal applications of lean in 1995.
Improvements, despite declining volumes nationwide due to email, includes:
1. Million square feet of space freed-up for consolidation, reducing reliance on leases.

2. 10 years of consecutive profitability.
3. Returned dividends to the Canadian government each year, including $59 million in 2005.
4. Reduced reliance on material handling equipment, overhead conveyors, forklifts, etc.
5. Dramatically reduced on-floor inventories, reducing lead-time, and improving quality.
6. Freed-up capacity and an increase in available machine time.
7. Improved labour relations; no labour disruptions since starting lean (The company said no one lost their employment because of lean.)

The Director of Logistics believes the company is at a new stage in its transformation. "We have left the phase of just making improvements in isolated pockets, and we are beginning to plan initiatives to improve companywide performance," he explained. "In other words, value-stream plans and hoshin kanri guide our initiatives, rather than isolated improvements. We are also on the verge of seeing lean become an embedded philosophy that will continue uninterrupted when the key champions leave or retire."

Chapter 18: Lean Methodologies in Public Libraries

In recent years, service industries have begun to adopt lean principles and experiment with the application of lean methods in service organizations. Many studies exist which focus on lean practises to improve workflow, increase production and service time, value the customer, and create an egalitarian work environment which continually strives for improvement. This chapter investigates the application of lean ideals in a North American public library environment.

There is very little books available pertaining directly to public libraries and lean methodologies. The majority of the books can be found in the business sector and focuses on lean methodologies to improve manufacturing and production. In terms of the service industry, majority of the books are about health care, financial and retail sectors adoption of lean practises..

Public libraries have traditionally featured a top down, hierarchical management style. Within this hierarchy, directives come from the library board and top management, cascading down through the ranks to the staff on the library floor. In keeping with lean principles, we will advocate a "participative management" style which "involves employees in sharing information, making decisions, solving problems, planning projects, and evaluating results".

Lean's people centred approach allows "decisions to be made by people closer to the action". Library management and staff must begin to envision the back room and reference and circulation desks as the gemba (Japanese term for where the work takes place), with all improvements and information originating from the gemba; thereby inverting the traditional pyramid and placing importance on the staff in the workplace.

Cross training in a lean environment could also be beneficial to public libraries. Ensuring that staff on all shifts are trained in all areas will limit the instances of work in progress (WIP) when staff are absent or on another shift. This will in turn increase turnaround time for new and returned materials as well as decrease touch times. Similarly, items needing repairs could be handled by more than one staff person instead of being shelved until the return of the staffer with such expertise. Cross training not only decreases WIP, it can also improve staff relations. The Grand Rapids Public Library discovered that "cross training has occurred so that people are able to back one another up as needed and keep materials flowing".

It is important to note that many public libraries are unionized environments. Employee unions must be involved in decisions pertaining to job descriptions and employee duties. Since many unionized manufacturing facilities have successfully adopted lean practises this should not prove an issue in unionized public libraries.

Workflow within public libraries is an area with the most potential for benefits from lean implementation. Initiatives such as kaizen events are a good starting point for organizations adopting lean practises. Within public libraries, staff would be organized into smaller teams in order to take part in these events. Initially, the event should feature a spaghetti map showing areas of workflow which are currently inefficient (resembling a bowl of cooked pasta). Teams then work together to create value stream maps (VSM) which feature more efficient standardized travel patterns for circulation duties, processing materials and back room tasks. Gemba walks involving management and staff walk-through to pinpoint problems and discuss solutions can easily be implemented in public libraries. Root cause analysis, in which employees evaluate the cause of problems and collectively create solutions, could also occur as a result of such events.

DMAIC (design, measure, analyse, improve and control) initiatives can also be implemented in various areas of library work. The Grand Rapids Public Library utilized DMAIC to improve their return processing times. Grand Rapids staff created value stream maps which reorganized workflow and limited touch times and posted them on white boards for all staff. Staff also standardized check-ins with a pre-sort by material type. In conjunction with the lean initiative FIFO (first in first out), staff eliminated back room shelving to limit time between materials being returned and appearing on the library floor. Instead, wheeled pre-labelled return carts were created which are returned to the floor for browsing.

In keeping with lean principles, supermarket or storage areas and water spiders (a person assigned to circulate between the gemba and supermarket) can also be created in library back rooms. The supermarket area holds supplies, clearly labelled and foot-printed. Foot-printing involves marking boxes with their location and contents and drawing an outline around the item to limit confusion or incorrect stocking. Water spiders on all shifts would be responsible for ensuring supplies are full at the beginning of each shift. These measures eliminate unnecessary time spent searching for pamphlets, labels, etc. while trying to serve customers.

Starbucks implementation of lean practises serves as an example to libraries. Starbucks' baristas moved items such as syrups and baked goods closer together and incorporated rolling racks to cut down on drink making times and steps taken, thereby increasing the number of customers served and decreasing time per transaction. Circulation and reference staff could move items frequently used closer together, such as new cards and de-magnetizers to improve work flow, decrease steps and improve staff health. A Starbucks outlet in downtown Chicago colour coded bins for different types of coffee beans and placed them on the counter instead of underneath to reduce back strain and bending time as well as limit errors and time spent reading labels. This outlet saw an increase in their customer satisfaction score from 56% to 76% and an increase in transactions of 9%.

One basic initiative to improve service in libraries involves the automation of circulation, printing and computer use. Libraries can increase customer independence, reduce wait times and theft, and free up staff time for larger issues, by implementing a card such as the Access Brooklyn Card. Brooklyn Public Library staff found that allowing borrowers to book computers, print copies and manage their own accounts with one card improved efficiency and saved time and money. Libraries experiencing chaos as a result of heavy computer and printer use or with limited staff would benefit from such a system.

Standardization of signage and fixtures can also be beneficial to service. Signs that are uniform in size and colour across branches allow customers to quickly find items and personnel. Self check out stations that are foot-printed at each location in a standard area will also allow customers to quickly and efficiently self serve if desired. Similarly, foot-printing pathways to various sections of the library (as can be found in hospitals and retailers such as IKEA) will increase self service, thereby freeing up staff for more involved reference questions and improved customer service.

Reducing wait times and errors, and increasing efficiency as a result of better work flow and ergonomically correct practises will positively affect customer service. More staff will be available to assist customers thereby reducing wait times, independent customers will have the ability to quickly serve themselves, and more materials will be available as they will be processed in a timely manner. A happier, healthier staff will pass on the numerous benefits of working in a lean environment to their satisfied customers.

Chapter 19: The Lean Approach

Case Study: How lean contributes to the improvement of Saskatchewan.

Words: Lean Program Manager, City of Saskatchewan

Saskatchewan is a province with a medium population in the country of Canada which is located in the continent/region of North America. Its biggest cities and towns include Saskatoon, Regina, Prince Albert and Moose Jaw.

Lean is a business technique used to improve the way we work. The Lean approach identifies and eliminates unnecessary steps, streamlines processes and ultimately improves value for the end users; our clients and customers.

The Lean approach works because it invites collaboration between employees responsible for carrying out the work, customers, and other stakeholders along the way. All of these groups provide input to ensure a smooth process to deliver goods and services.

The Government of Saskatchewan province has introduced Lean to continuously improve its service delivery to the public. Employees around the province are embracing the Lean way of thinking to improve systems and processes, and to streamline their work.

Why Lean?

Lean is intended to increase customer/client service and operational capacity. The term "Lean" refers to a basic absence of waste. It's not an acronym.

We believe the Lean initiative will help improve our service to the people of Saskatchewan. It's a business philosophy that has proven time and again that it works to improve processes.

What distinguishes Lean from other improvement efforts?

Three things:
1. Focus on the client or customer, and what they value, in order to reduce or eliminate waste.
2. Engagement of employees to seek ways to work better and smarter; no one knows a process better than the front line staff directly involved in it.
3. Rapid improvement. Lean process has been proven to deliver rapid results. Depending on the commitment to the work required, employees can start to make improvements in as little as a couple of months.

Is Lean being used to cut positions? Is it part of the workforce adjustment strategy?

No, Lean is not tied to workforce adjustment. Lean is not about job cuts or reducing the size of government, it's about improving the way we do our work and providing better services to the people of the province. Savings in time and money that are identified through Lean are reinvested back into the system, which creates even more value from a taxpayer perspective.

Is there an end date to Lean?

No. The Government of Saskatchewan is working toward establishing a culture of Lean in our workplace. This means that, eventually, all managers and employees will understand the concepts and methodology of Lean, and can apply them in their daily work.

Is this only for Ministries that deliver service to the public?

No, Lean is being incorporated into work throughout the public service, in all ministries and in addition to the Saskatchewan Liquor and Gaming Association, Water Security Agency, and Saskatchewan Crop Insurance Corporation. As well, Lean is being introduced into the education and post-secondary education sectors and Lean has been playing an integral role throughout the province's health sector for a number of years.

What is the support for Lean within the Government of Saskatchewan?

Premier Brad Wall is very supportive of the Lean initiative, and frequently references Lean successes in speaking engagements and in government materials.

In addition, a Minister Responsible for Lean has been established to ensure oversight and guidance on the program into the future.

Is there an overall governance structure for Lean in the public service?

Yes, Lean in the Saskatchewan public service is overseen by a formal committee of deputy ministers called the Lean Governance Steering Committee.

In addition, the steering committee is supported by the Ministry of Education's Corporate Projects Group, which is responsible for providing central oversight of the Lean initiative across the public service.

What is the interest in Lean from other jurisdictions?

Other public sector jurisdictions across North America are very interested in learning more about Saskatchewan's advances using Lean. They recognize that we are one of the first public sector workplaces to incorporate the methodology, and the first public sector workplace to incorporate it across the public service.

Chapter 20: Lean Terminologies

Lean is not a familiar terminology in Government; therefore it is prudent to conclude this book by explaining what some of the commonly use lean terminology means.

What is a VSM?

VSM stands for **value stream mapping**. A VSM is typically a day to a week-long event that enables a team of employees, managers, and often clients to take an in-depth look at a workplace processes and determine improvements that could be made. Nothing is taken for granted, and every aspect of a work process is questioned. Work during a VSM includes problem solving and physical transformation of the process.

You've likely seen the meeting rooms of people with sticky notes across the walls. Those sticky notes are the "map" of the process being discussed; every action that is undertaken within a process. Each one is examined during the VSM and questioned to determine relevance. The initial VSM meeting/initiative will end when a new process map is created (more sticky notes on the walls!) and a plan to move forward is created.

What is a Kaizen?

Sometimes not all issues or challenges can be resolved through a VSM, and so further events, called Kaizens, are initiated. A Kaizen is an incremental improvement that will help a VSM team continue with continuous improvement. Think of it as a smaller VSM, and a necessary part of the larger outcome. Key elements of a Kaizen include simplifying tasks and making them easier to perform; increasing the speed and efficiency of a work process; maintaining a safe work environment; and constantly improving quality.

What is 5S?

5S is a philosophy and tool to simplify, clean up, and organize a workplace and work materials in order to reduce waste and optimize quality and productivity. By maintaining an orderly workplace for work materials, standardizing work, and using visual cues, employees are able to achieve more consistent results. A well-ordered, effective workplace, including work materials and work products, is the foundation of improvement. 5S stands for; sorting, set in order, systematic cleaning, standardizing, and sustaining.

What is Hoshin?

Goals (with targets) and the means for achieving them in order to address business priorities to move the organization to a new level of performance; variable from year-to-year; could also be multi-year; and is developed by executive management.

What is a Lean Leader?

Each ministry, agency or crown has designated one or more people to be Lean Leaders in the workplace.

These Lean Leaders are responsible for delivering introductory Lean orientation, providing advice to senior leaders and Lean Deployment Champions, and helping to facilitate a culture of Lean. They are also responsible for leading teams through VSM and Kaizen events.

What is a Lean Deployment Champion?

A Lean Deployment Champion provides leadership and drives Lean within a ministry, agency or crown. He or she is responsible for establishing governance (such as a Lean Steering Committee) in the organization, and develops a Lean deployment strategy, which will include selection of VSMs, staff engagement, improvement targets and a training strategy. The Deployment Champion also reports progress to the Deputy Minister/Executive and to the Lean Steering Committee.

What is A3 Thinking?

A3 Thinking underpins business improvement culture. The A3 Thinking approach offers organizations a systematic method for realizing opportunities for improvement in the workplace.

A3 Thinking has been repeatedly reported to be a key tool in Toyota's quality-focused history. This simple process has underpinned Toyota's continual improvement program, delivering accelerated efficiency and other quality-related benefits.

The A3 reporting process itself only reflects half of the story. The development of an improvement and change-focused company culture is at the core of A3 Thinking. The deployment of an A3 reporting process in an organization enables a company-wide improvement culture to flourish.

A3 Thinking offers many advantages.

The A3 approach offers the following key features:
1. Provides a logical thinking process.
2. Clearly presents known information objectively.
3. Focuses on and shares critical information.
4. Aligns effort with strategy/objectives.
5. Provides a consistent approach throughout the organization.
6. Provides a powerful problem solving process.

A3 paper reports.

Traditionally, A3 reports are so named because they fitted onto one side of an A3-sized sheet of paper (about 11×17 inches). The purpose was to document and show on one page the results from the PDCA (Plan-Do-Check-Act) cycle.

The A3 report process aligns to and supports Deming's 'Plan-Do-Check-Act' management philosophy. PDCA is often used in business for the control and continuous improvement of processes and products.

What is PDCA cycle?

Plan
Establish the objectives and processes necessary to deliver results in accordance with the expected output (the target or goals).

Do
Implement the plan, execute the process, make the product. Collect data for charting and analysis in the Check and Act steps.

Check
Study the actual results (measured and collected in the Do stage above) and compare against the expected results (targets or goals from the Plan) to ascertain any differences.

Act
Request corrective actions on significant differences between actual and planned results. Analyze the differences to determine their root causes.

A3 Thinking provides a logical improvement workflow

The basic A3 Thinking workflow is shown below:
1. Plan: Project title.
2. Plan: Form the team.
3. Plan: Define current condition.
4. Plan: Define the goal.
5. Plan: Root cause analysis.
6. Do: Deploy countermeasures.
7. Check: Effective confirmation.

8. Act: Follow-up actions.
9. Act: Document changes and report.

As you can see, the A3 process is weighted towards planning. It is important to understand what we are doing before attempting to solve the problem. All effort invested into the planning phase will reduce mistakes and improve the final results.

An intuitive A3 workflow framework. A3 steps described in more detail below.

1. Plan: Select an A3 project title.

It's important to select a descriptive and useful project title or theme. For example, it might be "Reduce sensor failures" or "Improving on-time delivery". The theme should focus on the problem observed, describing this particular A3 project's purpose.

2. Plan: Form the team.

Select a team that includes process stakeholders. Process owners and operators are often the people most equipped to improve it, so the bulk of the team should comprise of these people. Include improvement coaches and technical experts as required. Teams can range from 1-20 depending on the project's requirements.

3. Plan: Define current condition

Outline the current situation in a simple way for the target audience. Be objective and state all the relevant known facts. Think about including charts, tables, graphs or using other techniques to illustrate the current condition. Think "communication".

4. Plan: Define the goal

Define the desired condition. How we will know that the project is successful at the end of the implementation? For example: "Our goal is to reduce sensor failures by 80% versus 2013 results".

5. Plan: Root cause analysis

Describe the Root-Cause Analysis investigation. How was the root-cause of the problem identified? Use the seven basic quality tools as required, list what was used and the results.
    a. The cause-and-effect chart (a.k.a. "fishbone" or Ishikawa diagram).
    b. The check sheet.
    c. The control chart.
    d. The histogram.
    e. The Pareto chart.
    f. The scatter diagram.
    g. Stratification (alternatively, flow chart or run chart)

6. Do: Deploy countermeasures

The Countermeasures section is focused on improvement planning. List the actions and tasks for tackling the problem. This section also serves as an action plan that outlines who will do what, by when.

This section can also list other A3 projects that have been identified.

7. Check: Effective confirmation

Define a method for assessing if the countermeasures have been successful. What is the difference between the desired condition and the improvements made through our current countermeasures? Did the countermeasures have an effect, or not?

8. Act: Follow-up actions

Here we reflect what further changes should be made to the system to sustain the improvement and what remains to be done. This could be further process changes or requesting entirely new A3 projects.

9. Act: Document changes and report

It is always important to correctly document all improvement work as this helps future improvement activity. For significant projects think about creating a project case study slide. Always ensure projects are properly closed down following completion. Also, list all updated documents, processes and procedures in this section.

The A3 Thinking process requires a pipeline of ideas from the workforce, customer and business strategy.

A3 thinking supports an improvement-focused culture. The A3 process empowers all employees to realize improvements and solve problems themselves.

It is very important to install a workforce-wide Opportunities Database to provide an ongoing supply of improvement opportunities. If the workforce is able to realize improvements quickly then a continuous supply of new ideas needs to be maintained.

Good Luck!!

www.ingramcontent.com/pod-product-compliance
Lightning Source LLC
Chambersburg PA
CBHW051708170526
45167CB00002B/586